Love Over Religion

Love Over Religion

Why I left Christianity

Danica Allen

ISBN-13: 9781974289035
ISBN-10: 1974289036

Chapters

Intro...

when a polite goodbye won't behave.

Dear Reader,

Many months ago, this began as a personal correspondence to answer the question, "Why did you leave Christianity?" I knew I would be faced with the question, sooner or later. I also knew the question would come from somebody I cared about, somebody who had supported me on my life journey. I decided to write this letter, rather than risk an argument or a discussion that might drive a painful wedge between us. I would then keep a copy and give it not just to one person, but to anyone who asked. It would be my readily-available damage control. It would be nonconfrontational, maybe even superficial, and five pages at best.

Three months later and 30 pages in, I realized the breadth and weight of the subject matter. This was not just a polite goodbye, a cursory pamphlet to tack onto the end of an email, whereby magically I could make my graceful exit from the belief system that burdened me for 10 years. Christianity had hurt me. I needed to be transparent about that, even with myself.

Christian messages, seemingly benign, were harming other people as well. My letter became an opportunity to speak up for those people. It became less about myself, about sustaining my relationships and keeping the peace. I now understood that my story could be an encouragement for anyone who is facing the very real challenges of leaving a religion. It could be an asset to those who have never subscribed to religion, if they chose to explain their choices to religious friends and family members. It could even be a resource for Christians who honestly yearn to understand why some people reject religion. One thing is for certain, though...

It is not five pages. And it is not going to make people love me.

If you allow me to share my story with you, you will learn that I did not "walk out on God" over a scuffle with a church leader, or because of a pain point with one or two politically-charged verses. My choice to leave Christianity was multifaceted and well-researched. Before making this decision, I spent 10 years regularly attending a variety churches (from Catholic, to Pentecostal, and everything in-between). I took college courses in world religion and independently studied the Bible and Christianity. I had, if you will, a "personal relationship with Jesus." I prayed, sang on the worship team, and participated in Bible studies.

As you will soon unfold, my years of Christianity did not provide the joy, the peace, and the life answers that I was hoping for. My studies led me to the conclusion that the nature of the Judeo-Christian God presented a conflict. If the Bible was true, then its God was not worth my respect or my praise, and the principles of Christianity were not suitable guidelines for my life. In this letter, I will explore the many reasons I left Christianity, including Biblical paradoxes, current and historical issues, and subjective personal concerns. I will also share some feelings that accompany leaving a religion, both the painful and the very liberating.

Whether you are Christian, or atheist, or find yourself somewhere in the middle, I have written this letter for you. Its purpose is to build a bridge between us, and not a wall. It will be brutally honest at times, but it is tender at its core. I hope that, throughout it, I have honored our differences and cherished our bonds. My only intention is to engage in a conversation with you. I hope that this conversation, like the best of them, will include laughter, some tears, and just a few unanswered questions so that it won't be our last.

Would you forgive me if I brought up something as seedy as politics, to kick us off?

The Lewd and the Rude...
why does God have a potty mouth?

In 2017, the United States of America elected Donald Trump as our new president. He follows President Obama, who had a reputation for honoring America's rich diversity during his time in office. In contrast, Trump made several statements that indicated bigotry, homophobia, and misogyny. The fact that he won the election came as a surprise to many. Trump was supported, in large part, by the Christian right. This also came as a surprise being that, on the surface, some of his words and actions did not appear to reflect Christian morality. For example, before running for president, he mentioned grabbing a woman by her—well, we all know what he said. Trump later dismissed the relevance of his remarks, calling them "locker room banter."[1]

I'm a rational person. I'm sure Donald Trump is not the first man to use locker room speech, though I would never assume this is the norm. Regardless, what differentiates Trump from a "regular guy," is the fact that he is now in the position of leading our nation, half of which comprises women, mothers, daughters, grandmothers. His sexist statements reflect poorly on him, especially now, in that role of leadership. Eloquent speech that displays integrity, honor, and compassion is something Americans generally seek in presidential candidates. But at the end of the day, even presidents are human beings. I'm sure we agree that there is no perfect person.

The interesting thing is, his comments were much more Christian in nature than I originally perceived. In fact, the God of the universe, the one we have elected into the highest place of power, uses locker room banter that would put Trump to shame.

> Behold, I am against you, says the Lord of hosts, and will lift up your skirts over your face; and I will let nations look on your nakedness and kingdoms on your shame. I will throw filth at you and treat you with contempt, and make you a gazingstock. (Nahum 3:5-6)

> ...That is why you have been stripped and raped by invading armies. (Jeremiah 13:22)

> I myself will strip you and expose you to shame. (Jeremiah 13:26)

> You built yourself a high place, at the top of every street and made your beauty abominable, and you spread your legs to every passer-by, to multiply your harlotry. (Ezekiel 16:25)

Adonai will strike the crown of the heads of Tziyon's women with sores, and Adonai will expose their private parts. (Isaiah 3:17)

And I will not have mercy upon her children, for they be the children of whoredoms. (Hosea 2:4)

Their conduct was like a woman's monthly uncleanliness, in my sight. (Ezekiel 36:17)

And your children shall wander in the wilderness forty years, and bear your whoredoms, until your carcasses be wasted in the wilderness. (Numbers 14:33)

They will leave you stark naked, and the shame of your prostitution will be exposed…and you will tear your breasts. I have spoken, declare the Sovereign Lord." (Ezekiel 23:28-34)

Almost every time god gets "mad" he uses dehumanizing "locker room speech" directly humiliating to women, as a metaphor. He proudly announces that he will rape someone that displeases him by worshipping another god. If a song came on the radio with lyrics like this, I would change the station, based solely on the offensive nature of the language. So why would I read, or encourage my child to read "The Good Book?" Why is something that is supposed to be godly in nature, full of so many offensive and base remarks?

Let me play devil's advocate here. (Not literally, relax!) If a man engages in locker room banter once or twice, I wouldn't judge his entire character on it. He might be a wonderful father, an excellent husband, a caring citizen, a merciful leader. So what's a little potty mouth, if he's getting the job done, and no one is getting hurt in the process?

For the sake of argument, let's give him the benefit of the doubt. Let's forgive the Biblical God his lewd comments, and fast forward from the morally ambiguous...

to the morally abhorrent.

God Murders Children...
and he thinks you should too.

Though many Christians of today are pro-life, their creator (according to the Bible) certainly was not. He proudly talks about killing unborn children and future children, as well as the living. He describes ripping open the wombs of women. If this alone were not disturbing enough, he describes taking pleasure in it, to draw attention to his own power.

> And I will cause them to eat the flesh of their sons and the flesh of their daughters. (Jeremiah 19:9) **[Cannibalistic verses like this are quite numerous in the Bible. Ew.]**

> If thy son or thy daughter…entice thee secretly saying, "Let us go and serve other gods"…thou shalt surely kill him…thou shalt stone him with stones, that he die. (Deuteronomy 13:6-10)

> If a man have a stubborn and rebellious son…all the men of his city shall stone him with stones, that he die. (Deuteronomy 21:18-21) **[It's okay to kill your children, according to the Bible, even for something pretty**

common. **Kids are stubborn. It's surprising any of them made it past the terrible twos!**]

Now therefore, kill every male among the little ones [**boy children**] and kill every woman that hath known man by lying with him. [**But little virgin girls can be saved, presumably to rape them, eventually? Logic and historical context would concur.**] (Numbers 31:17)

Their infants shall be dashed in pieces, and their women with child shall be ripped up. (Hosea 13:16) [**This is abortion.**]

Now go and smite Amalek, and utterly destroy all that they have, and spare them not, but slay both man and woman, *infant and suckling*, ox and sheep, camel and ass. (I Samuel 15:2-3) [**This is God directly and unambiguously ordering his followers to murder infants.**]

I will punish the world for its evil...Whoever is found will be thrust through, and whoever is caught will fall by the sword. Their infants will be dashed to pieces before their eyes, their houses will be plundered, and their wives ravished...they will have no mercy on the fruit of the womb; their eyes will not pity children. (Isaiah 13:11-18)

Happy shall they be who take your little ones and dash them against the rock. (Psalm 137: 8-9) [**This is literally**

disgusting to me, as it describes taking pleasure in beating babies against a rock]

Ephraim's glory will fly away like a bird. No birth, no pregnancy, no conception. Even if they rear children, I will bereave them of every one…Ephraim will bring out their children *to the slayer.* (Hosea 9:11-13)

Incredibly, I used to justify these verses by concluding that they were metaphors. Upon careful read, God is *directly and unambiguously* ordering his followers to murder children, threatening to keep women from conceiving or to open their wombs and kill their fetuses, or even kill their children once born.

———

The widely-accepted tradition of Passover, which Jesus himself celebrated, commemorates God's murder of thousands.

On that night, I will pass through the land of Egypt, and strike down every firstborn son…And that night, at midnight, the Lord struck down all the firstborn sons in the land…there was not a single house where someone had not died. (Exodus 13:12-28)

———

Whether it happened or was (more obviously) fictional, religion has warped murder into a celebration. Most loving followers of the Jewish and Christian religions would never consider Passover from this perspective. Herein is evidence that religion poisons the mind. Religious tradition reduces the ability to discern objectively. There are millions of people worldwide who celebrate annually the salvation of those whom death "passed over," and ignore the concurrent genocide of those whom it did not. Wouldn't that be the same as survivors celebrating the Holocaust, because they, personally, had not perished in it?

In the context of religion, since the "believers" were not harmed, the death and sorrow that befell "non-believers" is not only permissible, but is celebrated. And speaking of non-believers, is it okay to enslave them? And how about raping them, while we're at it? Check out the following chapter, to see how the Biblical God would respond to those questions.

God Encourages Slavery and Rape...
but don't go to church without a hat!

Slavery is one of the most horrific evils that have plagued our world. To me, there is nothing more disturbing than sex slavery, or child slavery. As such, it shocks and perturbs me that the Biblical God of the universe condones slavery, including sex and child slavery. God's followers were commanded to invade tribes, kill men and take children and women to do with as they pleased. In one of the best-known segments of the Bible, the Ten Commandments, God writes a law that prohibits *the coveting* of slaves, but not *the owning* of slaves! In other words, it's fine to own slaves, as long as you're not envious of your neighbor's slaves. Wow. I'd like to fantasize that some primitive version of autocorrect botched that one, but the Bible is consistent. Even Jesus, who put an end to many of the harmful practices in the Old Testament ignored his chance to end slavery. In fact, in the New Testament we read, "Slaves, obey your earthly masters with deep respect and fear." (Ephesians 6:5) Almost 2,000 years after God came to Earth to teach us right from wrong, "upstanding" Christian citizens in the United States felt entitled to own slaves because the Bible endorsed it. The Bible never changed its mind on slavery. It was only when people began to listen to their own conscience and moral code that, at last, slavery was abolished here.

I know. I know. "But we don't believe *that* part of the unchanging word of God."

Anyone who beats their male or female slave with a rod must be punished if the slave dies as a direct result. But they are not to be punished if the slave recovers after a day or two, since the slave is their property. (Exodus 21:20)

If a man has a sexual relationship with a woman who is a slave, designated for another man...he shall bring a guilt offering for himself...and the sin he committed shall be forgiven him. **[Sounds pretty easy. Thanks, God!]** (Leviticus 19:20-22)

As you approach a town to attack it, you must first offer its people terms for peace. If they accept your terms, and open the gates to you, then all the people inside will serve you in forced labor. But if they refuse to make peace **[or become your slaves]** and prepare to fight, you must attack the town. When the Lord your God hands the town over to you, use your swords to kill every man in the town. But you may keep for yourselves all the women, children, livestock, and *other* plunder. You may enjoy the *plunder* from your enemies that the Lord your God has given you. (Deuteronomy 21: 10-14) **[I cringe**

when I imagine how God's people "enjoyed" those women and children, or as God disparagingly refers to them, "plunder."]

Behold. I have two daughters who have not yet known man. Let me bring them out to you, and do to them as you please. Only do nothing to these men, for they have come under the shelter of my roof. (Genesis 19:7-8) **[Very disturbing that a father would hand over his daughters to be raped, in order to defend total strangers—males, of course. To affirm that God looked favorably on this proposed rape, Lot was spared while the city burned.]**

When thou goest forth to war against thine enemies… and seest among the captives a beautiful woman and hast a desire unto her…bring her home to thine house…and after that, thou shalt go into her and be her husband. (Deuteronomy 21:10-13) **[This is rape]**

Do not deprive each other of sexual relations, unless you both agree to refrain from sexual intimacy. (I Corinthians 7:5) **[This could also be construed as rape. If one party does not consent, it is rape. Here sex is permitted if one person doesn't desire it, as long as <u>both</u> parties haven't agreed to refrain.]**

The wife does not have authority over her own body, but yields it to her husband. In the same way, the husband does not have authority over his own body, but yields it to his wife. (1 Corinthians 7:4)

The United States Department of Justice defines rape as: *the penetration, no matter how slight, of the vagina or anus with any body part or object, or oral penetration by a sex organ of another person, without the consent of the victim.* [2] To me, that sounds a lot like not having authority over your body. Apparently, I'm not the only one who interprets these verses as, "It's okay to rape your wife." In your spare time, check out the online article "Biblical Gender Roles. Is my Husband Raping me?"[3] Grab a barf bag, first.

————

The National Coalition Against Domestic Violence reports that 10-14 percent of women are raped by their husbands. Eighteen percent of these victims report that their children witnessed the rape.[4] Women with religious beliefs are less likely to report these incidences, or remove themselves from the abusive relationship, as they believe they are "obliged" to have sex with their husbands, and they fear divorce and the punishment from God that ensues.[5]

————

Very simply put, it is sex when both parties agree. It is rape when one party is forced to submit because her partner, her captor, or her God tells her she must. The Bible condones rape. Even if your personal interpretation of these verses differs, women have been raped because of them.

If you happen to be of the camp that firmly believes God never changed his mind on homosexuality, guess what? He never changed his mind on rape or slavery either. The Old and New Testaments consistently condone both. If the Bible is the clear and unchanging word of God, we cannot twist and shape it to excuse parts of it, while vehemently upholding others.

If homosexuality, extramarital sex, or divorce is a sin, it is an equal sin for Christian women to teach in church.

> Women should remain silent in the churches. They are not allowed to speak, but must be in submission, as the law says. (I Corinthians 14:34) **[Most churches completely disregard this verse.]**

It is also a sin for women to go to church without a hat on.

> If a woman does not cover her head, let her hair be cut off. (I Corinthians 11:6)

It is a sin to marry a divorced woman.

> Whoever shall marry her that is divorced, committeth adultery. (Matthew 5:32)

If the argument is that the Bible is the unchanging word of God, then we cannot pick and choose which parts of it are unchanging. Many Christians completely blow over entire segments of the Bible that are outdated, such as God's full-on blessing to buy, own, rape, and sell slaves. But when referring to homosexuality or extramarital sex, these same Christians stand confidently on their pulpit, Bible in hand, and profess that God's word is the ultimate truth. It never changes. It never fails. The same pastors whose wives teach in church (also strictly prohibited by the Bible!) would allow their own children to suffer and believe they are going to hell if their sexual path is not "Biblical."

Gay teenagers are two to three times more likely to take their own lives[6], and most Christians believe they have license to condemn homosexuals, because "God does." How is this any different than supporting slavery because the Bible says it's okay? This is a clear example of refusing to listen to one's conscience, and relying on a religious text to decipher right from wrong. Passively supporting the discrimination against gay people is like physically punching a child that's already being bullied, or adding degrading comments to a cyberbullying thread. It is pushing an already vulnerable child one step closer to taking their own life.

Can you imagine a child feeling so burdened, so overwhelmed that the only relief they can imagine is dying? Can you imagine believing God created you, but does not love or accept the real you? Wondering if the only solution is ending your own life, and if so, whether you will then suffer in eternal hell? If you are on the Christian side of this argument, you may believe you are showing people love by "hating their sin." If this is where you are, I would encourage you to shift your paradigm and understand that what you are showing the marginalized is not love but passive hatred, passive bullying. It is every bit as destructive, damaging, and unforgettable. In fact, Christian rejection of homosexuals can be even more painful than other forms of bullying. The Christian message comes across as, "I love you, but God will not love or accept you, unless you change who you are." How devastating that message can be, in the heart of an 11-year-old who is just beginning to understand the complexities of life. Efforts to reduce the bullying and discrimination against LGBTQ youth are often halted by Christians. This is literally fighting on the side of the bullies![7]

Maybe it just doesn't matter, until it's your child. Or maybe, it doesn't even matter then.

Such is indoctrination.

———

It is unacceptable for people who claim to have the love of God in their hearts to stand by while members of their human family are experiencing ridicule and discrimination.

———

Instead of respecting the individuality of others, many Christians spend time praying to save the souls of the "lost."

They ask God to change the hearts of people who think differently than they do. They believe they are loving people through these prayers. But while they are busy praying for a different version of someone, they missing out on the beautiful opportunity to know that person for who they really are.

There is never a good moment to address the abortion argument. I will make only one point, and I will do it in four sentences. (Hey, you've made it this far!) Regardless of your opinion on abortion, it is a fact that not all babies will be born heterosexual, American Christians. You do realize that some of those babies will grow up to be gay, lesbian, Muslim, Jewish, transgender, atheist, vegan, democratic. Here is one of the reasons people in favor of choice find it so difficult to lend credibility to the other side's argument: Many who claim to be pro-life can't even find it in their hearts to share the world with the people *that are already here.*

But like the Bible does, let's go back to slavery and rape!

Unfathomably, I used to defend the Bible's condoning of slavery and its lesser view of women and children as evidence that God was meeting the people where they were. I see that as nonsensical now. Remember, we're talking about God. He doesn't have to conform to the mistaken beliefs of human beings. His natural role would be to instruct us and correct us if we were doing things that were inhumane or cruel, not to participate in them.

Why would God draw out very specific laws regarding how hard slaves can be beaten, or when it's okay to rape a woman?

Sacrificing an innocent life to "appease God," is an ancient, tribal practice.[8] The fact that God sent his innocent son to die because the people were used to a blood atonement for sins does not speak to the loving and capable nature of God. He could very well have sent his son to teach us that sins can be forgiven without bloodshed. (Which, clearly, they can be. Or have you had to murder your pets, or your child, every time you forgive someone?)

The fact that our so-called "loving" God requested that people murder animals and spread their blood all over the temple to ask forgiveness (culminating in the pre-planned murder of his own son) means one of two things.

1. The Bible was not written by an omniscient, loving being who could clearly see how cruel and unnecessary it was to murder innocent beings in his honor. It was written by people who were evolving out of an aboriginal concept of religion, and who preserved many of the horrific practices of it. This seems like a logical, educated, and mature deduction, to me.

2. In the unlikely scenario number two, the Bible was indeed written by a spiritual entity. If this is true, it was written by a false god, an evil entity. It was written by a spirit of darkness, who wanted the massacre of innocents to continue. It would have to be a very dark soul, an entity with a nature that we would associate with our concept of Satan. It would be a devil who would ask his people to wring the neck of a beautiful, helpless dove, and sprinkle its blood on a religious temple, then burn another one to death. (Leviticus 6:8-10) It would be a demon who would suggest killing your family members, even your own child, if they refuse to worship him. (Deuteronomy 13:6-9)

————

Doesn't it sound demonic, to take pleasure in the smell of your dying child? (Ephesians 5:2)

————

Let's hope that the Bible is nothing more than a very ancient collection of laws and stories, primarily designed to coerce entire populations of people into submission. If this is not the case, and the Bible was indeed "divinely inspired" by some supernatural being, the only logical conclusion is that it was written by a demonic force. It was written to induce hatred and fear, justify massacres, encourage self-loathing, and perpetuate horrific crimes against human and animal life, throughout history and into current times.

If there were a good, loving god that decided to send an entire book to Earth, what might that book contain? Remember, this is God. He is not confined by historical context, or the limits of human understanding. He does not have to support slavery, just because the people of a particular era do. He could easily explain that slavery is horrific and unjust, and should be stopped immediately.

He doesn't have to warn people that touching a woman on her period will make them unclean, or that giving birth to a baby girl makes the mother unclean for a longer time than giving birth to a baby boy would. He would not dedicate verses to this, because he is God and he knows these aren't facts. In fact, he would probably spend some extra verses getting people up to speed on "girl stuff," so they would stop discriminating against women.

I'm guessing he also wouldn't dedicate chapter upon chapter to building temples in his name, and listing the many people that weren't perfect enough, or beautiful enough to even get near those temples. Doesn't seem very godlike, does it? More like a pompous, Hollywood diva. God, if there is one, is not vain. He is loving, and humble. He wants people to know how much more important it is to give their hearts to him, than build a temple.

I bet God would also include some really important stuff, like don't abuse children. Don't invade foreign countries, kill ruthlessly, or take slaves. Don't applaud murders. (David, a Biblical hero, killed tens of thousands of people, according to the Bible.) Be respectful of the Earth. It is a gift, and its resources are limited. Teach your children to love others as they are. Extend kindness to animals. They, too, have feelings.

Maybe God would even spruce it up with some little-known facts, like "Someday Alexa will play songs for you, and you will have a smartphone on which to watch cat videos." I would do that. If I were God.

Instead, the Bible is filled with very "ungodly" teachings. God's followers were told to invade for me! Kill for me! Destroy for me! Because people were following the "word of God," they couldn't hear their own conscience telling them these things were wrong. All these thousands of years later, *we're still doing it.*

But why? Why do some of us choose to ignore the voice of goodness inside of us, in favor of a cruel, ancient belief system? For many, it is because we're afraid of this vindictive, angry, and dangerous god. Compiled with that fear, we believe ourselves to be born sinners, useless lumps of clay, undeserving of life. These messages are repeated, over and over, in Christian sermons, and eventually they seep into the subconscious.

These also happen to be two key components in an abusive relationship. First, the abuser convinces you that you are worthless and helpless without him. Then he threatens horrible punishments if you leave him, but offers gleaming promises if you stay. Because you are beaten down and assume yourself inept, it makes sense to believe these threats and promises. In fact, emotional abuse and Biblical messages have some uncanny commonalities which I will soon explore in detail with you.

God is a Jealous, Angry, Abusive Father...
he must love you so much.

If my husband beat my children for something I did, I would leave him. If I heard of someone beating their children for something their grandparents did, I would report it to the police. Wouldn't you? Yet time and time again, the Judeo-Christian god threatens to punish innocent children for the "sins" of their fathers.

> I, the Lord, am a jealous God, visiting the iniquity of the fathers upon the children unto the third and fourth generation of them that hate me. (Deuteronomy 5:9)

> I will put an end to the arrogance of the haughty... their infants will be dashed to pieces before their eyes, their houses will be looted, and their wives violated. (Isaiah 13:11-16) **[Try imagining your own family members' names in this verse, as we often do with nicer verses.]**

> Your nakedness shall be uncovered, and your shame shall be seen. I will take vengeance, and I will spare no

man. Our Redeemer—the Lord of Hosts is his name—
is the Holy one of Israel. (Isaiah 47-3-4) **[More rape.
More murder. Yours truly, the Redeemer.]**

To stir up wrath and take revenge, I put her blood on
the bare rock, so that it would not be covered. (Ezekiel
24:8)

He will totally destroy them. He will give them over to
slaughter. Their slain will be thrown out. Their dead
bodies will stink. The mountains will be soaked with
their blood. (Isaiah 34:2-3)

I gave them statutes that were not good, and ordi-
nances by which they could not have life, and I defiled
them through their very gifts, in making them offer by
fire all their first born, that I might horrify them. I did
it that they might know that I am the Lord. (Ezekiel
20:25-26) **[Horrible. Let's read it again, different
version.]**

I gave them over to worthless decrees and regula-
tions that would not lead to life. I let them pollute
themselves with the very gifts I had given them, and
I allowed them to give their firstborn children as
offerings to their gods, so I might devastate them and
remind them that I alone am the Lord. (Ezekiel 20:20-
26) **[This is not how you reconcile the lost. This is an**

abusive authoritative figure. It's also another clear example of God condoning the murder of innocent children.]

In Judges we read the disturbing story of a man who promises to sacrifice a human being, if God grants him victory in battle. God proceeds to grant him the victory and, in what seems an evil twist of events, allows Jephthah to kill his own daughter as she runs out to greet him. Does God say, "No! Don't kill your only child, your loving and faithful daughter who has done no wrong?" Of course he doesn't. We get a window into the daughter's thoughts, as she begs only for time to mourn her approaching death, and the fact that she never had an opportunity to grow up and become a woman, a mother.

> Let this thing be done for me. Grant me two months, so that I may go and wander on the mountains, and bewail my virginity, my companions and I. (Judges 11:37)

Personally, I believe I shouldn't have to defend my disbelief in Christianity beyond this story. One dead child killed by her father should be enough. I can't support this belief system, and I won't pass it down to my own child. The horrific death of this innocent girl was commanded by the God Christians serve. And this story is void of morality, from start to finish.

What follows are some more illustrative words from the God Christians believe we will spend eternity with. Hmmm, I'm not so sure I want to! In fact, I have officially ripped this page out of my Bible, and I intend to read it if I need a reminder that a loving Judeo-Christian God is a myth.

> The Lord himself will send on you curses, confusion, and frustration in everything you do, until at last you are completely destroyed for doing evil and abandoning me. …The Lord will strike you with wasting diseases, fever, and inflammation, with scorching heat and drought, and with blight and mildew. These disasters will pursue you until you die…your corpses will be food for all the scavenging birds and wild animals…The Lord will afflict you with the boils of Egypt, and with tumors, scurvy, and the itch, from which you cannot be cured. The Lord will strike you with madness, blindness, and panic. You will grope around in broad daylight like a blind person groping in the darkness, but you will not find your way. You will be oppressed and robbed continually, and no one will come to save you. You will be engaged to a woman, but another man will sleep with her. (Deuteronomy 28:20-31)

[This goes on and on, but I won't bother typing it all here. Suffice it to say, it sounds nothing like the diplomatic and intelligent words of a loving father figure. In fact, it sounds everything like the ridiculous exaggerations of a petulant bully. This god is the bad guy in the

movie who is *SO* bad, he's almost laughable. He goes on with demeaning curses for a while, then goes back into a prime example of his support of child slavery.]

You will have sons and daughters, but you will lose them, because they will be led away into captivity. (Deuteronomy 28:41) **[God is willing to sell children into slavery, to punish people for not loving him quite enough.]**

To wrap it up, after this bounty of very poetic, borderline comedic curses, he says:

These horrors will serve as a sign and a warning among you and your descendants forever. If you do not serve the Lord your God with joy and enthusiasm for the abundant benefits you have received, you will serve your enemies whom the Lord will send against you. You will be left hungry, thirsty, naked, and lacking in everything. The Lord will put an iron yoke on your neck, oppressing you harshly until he has destroyed you. (Deuteronomy 28:46-48) **[Wow. After two pages of curses, he demands servitude with joy and enthusiasm? Just in time to continue with more curses.]**

If you refuse to obey all the words of instruction that are written in this book, and if you do not fear the glorious and awesome name of the Lord your God, then the Lord will overwhelm you and your children **[innocent children]** with indescribable plagues. These plagues will be intense and without relief, making you miserable and unbearably sick...Just as the Lord has found great pleasure in causing you to prosper and multiply, the Lord will find *great pleasure* in destroying you. (Deuteronomy 28:58-63) **[This sick-minded god is actually enjoying watching innocent children waste away with indescribable pain and sickness, according to this book of the Bible.]**

Couple these horrendous threats with the very consistent underlying message throughout the Bible that we are worthless without God, and you have a perfect recipe to control and manipulate entire populations of people.

I've heard many sermons where the "fear" of God is explained away as being a healthy fear and respect, not actual fear. In fact it is *quite* clear that the Bible's intention was to instill actual fear. There is no other way to interpret all of the verses of curses we just read.

———

If anything has ever been written to instill fear, it is the Bible.

———

Fear of God, fear of hell, fear of making a mistake and having your children suffer for it, fear of listening to your own conscience, fear of displeasing God in any micro-decision you make throughout your daily life. Fear of an angry god is the prevalent sentiment throughout the Old Testament. You would be hard pressed to open it to any page and not find a threat **within minutes** of beginning to read. You would also be hard pressed to find a message of support, of love, of reassurance, of forgiveness, of tolerance. It's no wonder people are willing to set aside their own reasoning and be washed into total submission to words written on a page. Because like the abused wife, they are terrified. Terrified to speak, terrified to stand up for the innocent, terrified to even think for themselves.

Lord, throughout all the generations
You have been our home!
Before the mountains were born,
Before you gave birth to the earth and the world,
From beginning to end, you are God.

You turn people back to dust, saying,
"Return to dust, you mortals."
For you, a thousand years are as a passing day,
As brief as a few night hours.
You sweep people away like dreams that disappear.
They are like grass that springs up in the morning.
In the morning, it blooms and flourishes,
But by evening, it is dry and withered.
We wither beneath your anger.
We are overwhelmed by your fury.

You spread out our sins before you—
Our secret sins—and you see them all.
We live our lives beneath your wrath,
Ending our years with a groan.

(Psalm 90:1-9)

I wish I could say the Bible put up a good fight when I was researching it to write this letter. Sadly, I had only to open "God's Word" to find countless examples of why I no longer wish to be associated with Christianity. I didn't even have to look outside of the Bible, to make my decision. It was plain as day, when I read with discernment.

———

My number one reason for leaving Christianity is the Bible itself: the negative view of human life that it proposes, the cruelty it condones, and the degrading and insulting way it speaks to me and to the people I love.

———

I found an interesting article called, "30 Signs of Emotional Abuse."[9] I will take a look at 15 of these emotional abuse indicators, lining them up with Bible verses.

1. They humiliate you in front of other people. *I will pelt you with filth; I will treat you with contempt; I will make you a public spectacle.* (Nahum 3:6)

2. They regularly disregard your opinions. *Then he said to them all, "Whoever wants to be my disciple must deny themselves and take up their cross daily and follow me."* (Luke 9:23)

3. They use sarcasm to make you feel bad about yourself. *Go and cry out to the gods you have chosen. Let them save you when you are in trouble.* (Judges 10:14)

4. They accuse you of being too sensitive to their remarks. *Who are you to question my wisdom with your ignorant, empty words? Now stand up straight and answer the questions I ask you. Where were you when I made the world?* (Job 38:2-4)

5. They try to control you and treat you like a child. *Like newborn babies, crave spiritual milk, so that by it you may grow into salvation.* (1 Peter 2:2)

6. They chastise you for your behavior. *Then I will give full vent to my hostility. I myself will punish you seven times over for your sins.* (Leviticus 26:28)

7. You feel like you need permission to make decisions. *"The rebellious children are as good as dead," says the Lord, "those who make plans without consulting me, who form alliances without consulting my Spirit, that they may add sin to sin."* (Isaiah 30:1)

8. They try to control finances and how you spend money. *Will a mere mortal rob God?...Yet you rob me... in tithes and*

offerings. You are under a curse—your whole nation—because you are robbing me."(Malachi 3:8-9)

9. They belittle your accomplishments, hopes, and dreams. *For apart from me you can do nothing. If anyone does not remain in me, he is like a branch that is thrown away and withers. Such branches are gathered up, thrown into the fire, and burned.* (John 15:5)

10. They make you feel as though they are right and you are always wrong. *As the heavens are higher than the earth, so are my ways higher than your ways and my thoughts higher than your thoughts.* (Isaiah 55:9)

11. They resort to pouting or withdrawal to get what they want. *So when you spread out your hands in prayer, I will hide My eyes from you. Yes, even though you multiply prayers, I will not listen...*(Isaiah 1:15)

12. They point out your flaws, mistakes, and shortcomings. *But you do not realize that you are wretched, pitiful, poor, blind, and naked.* (Revelation 3:17)

13. They accuse you for things you know aren't true. *Surely I was sinful at birth, sinful from the time my mother conceived me.* (Psalm 51:5)

14. They can't tolerate others laughing at them. *Then the Lord said to Abraham, "Why did Sarah laugh...is anything*

too hard for the Lord?" Sarah was afraid, so she lied and said, "I did not laugh." But he said, "Yes, you did laugh." (Genesis 18:13-15)

15. They view you as an extension of themselves, rather than as an individual. *Now you are the body of Christ, and each one of you is a part of it.* (I Corinthians 12:27)

When I really examined the demeaning messages in the Bible, it became clear to me that Christianity employs a form of emotional abuse to gain and retain followers. Not surprisingly, the Bible refers to believers as the "bride of Christ." When God isn't happy with his followers, he disparagingly refers to them as "harlots," or a "cheating wife." The entire message of the Bible resonates very clearly with emotional abuse tactics used in unhealthy relationships.

When you ask a Christian how God displays his love for us in the Bible, the most commonly quoted verse is John 3:16, which begins, "For God so loved the world that he gave his only begotten son." However, reflecting on the nature of God throughout the Bible, I don't see his "gift" of Jesus as a loving act. He forces his own son to die, in order to forgive the sins of other people. I see this as one more item in an almost endless list of nonsensical and dreadful acts that God has perpetrated in the Bible.

––––––––

If you or I can forgive someone without bloodshed, so can God. It makes no sense to believe that innocent animals, babies, or children had to be murdered so God could forgive our sins.

––––––––

It's an aboriginal myth that blood needs to be shed to forgive iniquity, or guarantee God's blessing. No rational person in today's world would buy into such a ridiculous belief if it were not for religious indoctrination. Blood can't forgive your sins any more than killing a chicken can get you a better job. Belief in such things is voodoo, and superstition, and scary, and dangerous.

I won't suggest that the Bible has disproven God to me. It has only disproven itself as a reference, as the book that was divinely inspired by a loving God. The Bible and the Biblical God appear to be works of fiction, written by people who were doing their best to explain things they couldn't understand, and conquer a few nations while they were at it. There may be some form of God out there, but I don't believe any God could have the jealous, petty, egotistic, angry, lewd, unjust character portrayed in the Bible. I would personally bet that if a God figure is up there, he's shaking his head that such atrocities, both in thought and action, have been accredited to him and are perpetuated in his name.

But what about Jesus? The guy who came to teach peace and love.

I asked myself this question a lot, during my in-between days of leaving religion. I do so love the *idea* of Jesus, the Jesus I pictured as the original hippie. He was the loving, gentle figure gazing down from the paintings in my childhood bedroom. He was the rebel that wasn't afraid to speak up for the poor. He was the superhero featured in fun Sunday school songs. I wish so much that he didn't claim to be the cruel God of the Old Testament, the killer, the rapist, the elitist, un-hippie God.

But he did.

In other words, Jesus claims not just to support God, but to BE him. The very same God that commands the death of innocent children, and condones the rape of foreigners, and hurls curses for disobedience. He did not come to refute the religious teachings of the day, but to affirm them. He linked himself inextricably to the prejudice, bigotry, misogyny, and hatred portrayed by the God of the Old Testament. I wish that Jesus had been the person I adored, during my time as a Christian. But that person would have been fighting for the same things I'm fighting for—love, acceptance, equality, respect for others, and peace.

It just seems so simple. If I can love someone as they are, and forgive someone without asking for anything in return, how can God/Jesus not do that, on an even larger scale? From God, I would expect greater love than humans love. I would expect less anger than humans have. I would expect more tolerance than humans show. I would expect unconditional love. This is what Christians say their God shows, but God's "document" doesn't support it.

So, let me summarize the first four chapters of my argument. If my husband makes a few dirty jokes, I would probably brush it off as "locker room banter." I'd stick around if he was a good man, and a loving father. But if he raped a few neighbors, sold some kids into slavery, ripped open a pregnant woman or two, threw babies against rocks, threatened others like a bully, was constantly angry and vindictive, and ordered the death of innocent animals and children to appease his wrath, I would *probably* have to reconsider. Would you encourage me to stay in that relationship?

Philosophical Paradox...
if I had the power to stop one thing from happening.

The last few chapters were dedicated to the Biblical paradox of God, the textual evidence from within that, for me, proves Christianity false. Now I'd like to tackle a philosophical paradox, looking at some real-world evidence for my disbelief. The examples I'm about to provide are every bit as emotionally disturbing as the verses I quoted in the first segment, only intensified because they are true, current events. They attest to the non-existence of God as we conceive him to be, in the Judeo-Christian context.

**Please note that the following chapter will be graphic in nature, and difficult for some readers. **

In the Bible, God speaks to people directly, and many Christians still hold the belief that God speaks and sends messages to his followers, today. In any context outside of religion, such a thought would be considered whimsical at best, and perhaps even delusional. But for some reason, society has decided that it's okay for a bunch of grownups to base their decisions on the direction of an unearthly voice, speaking into their brains. **Does God speak, or send messages to his believers?**

If he does, it leads me to wonder about the case of a 10-year-old girl who was brutally raped several times by men the mother solicited, on purpose, to violate her. The final rape ended with a gruesome murder, while this innocent child pleaded for her life. Her mother watched, unfazed. This was a child that went to a Christian church. She was undoubtedly told the same things many churches tell their children. "God is with you, wherever you go." "God is a strong, mighty protector. Don't be afraid!" I'm sure the final moments of this child's life were made infinitely more horrible by the belief that God was sitting by and watching this happen to her, just like her mother was. God, that has the power to protect and defend, the ability to strike a person dead (Acts 5:1-9) for something as simple as a lie, did not stop the brutal and incomprehensibly painful rape, murder, and dismemberment of a beautiful, innocent, Christian child.

It was the belief that *he could*, however, that would be most emotionally damaging, in those horrific last moments. While I cannot attest directly to what this child felt and thought in her last moments, I have personally spoken to victims of abuse who were told that God was watching over them, even while these horrible things were happening. Because of what the living victims have shared with me, I can fairly extrapolate what the murdered have also felt. It is sheer devastation at their own insignificance in the heart of a *supposedly* loving God.

If God can't intervene and rescue them, then children shouldn't be taught that he can. This makes life a living hell for abused children. If God can intervene and doesn't, then I have absolutely no desire to spend my eternity in worship of such a cruel and heartless god.

Sometimes there's a case on the news so terrible that people respond to it by saying, "It almost makes you lose your faith in God." It sounds cliché but I did lose my faith, in large part, over cases like the ones in this chapter. It is impossible for me to believe that God would permit these horrendous things, having the ability to stop them. It would be like sitting in the room, watching it happen, and allowing it to continue. No sane person would ever permit it. This renders all sane people more compassionate and more powerful than God. So in essence, I lost my faith due not to these crimes themselves, but to the unresolvable paradox they presented when it came to God's character.

If there is a God, he's terrible at his job. I would never want my child to believe that God could prevent something bad from happening to her or another child, but would refuse to do so. I could never explain that God simply permits atrocities such as bullying, animal cruelty, child abuse. Or maybe "the devil" commits them, and God is incapable of preventing them. How could I possibly teach her that, while insisting that God is powerful, and mighty, and he sees everything, and his love is great?

I will never forget the story of this 10-year-old girl, nor the story of countless victims of abuse that God not only failed to rescue, but also *failed to defend in his Holy Word.*

———

There is not a single verse condemning the sexual or physical abuse of children in the Bible. (But six entire chapters on how to build the perfect temple, and sew the perfect garments, and make the perfect animal sacrifices.)

———

Adding literal insult to injury, if you have been abused, the typical Christian teaching is that bad things happened to you so that you can console others. I do agree that if you take it upon yourself to turn your own personal tragedy into something positive, that is heroic. However, if your God, or your church, or your religion explains away your tragedy as something acceptable because it will be beneficial to others, it makes more acute the sensation that you do not matter as a human being, that you are worthless.

I have never, personally, faced starvation, and yet I am fully capable of sympathizing with the starving, and have participated in efforts to alleviate starvation in other countries. It is not factual or logical to deduce that a person must suffer, in order to console someone who is suffering. Here the Bible gives us a superficial explanation of human suffering, one that is easy to believe when we need to make sense of it. However, if we dig deep, the implications of this message are troubling, not consoling.

I choose to believe that the negative things that happened to me sucked. If I opt to console others through my experiences, instead of drowning my angst in alcohol or drugs, that's a positive outcome. But it doesn't make it okay that bad things happened to me. *I still matter.*

But I haven't answered my question. Does God send messages to his believers?

Let's go back to the case of the 10-year-old victim. If God indeed sends messages to his followers, as portrayed in the Bible and believed true by current Christians, why did he not bother to send a message to any one of the members of the Christian church where this child attended? Does this mean that while God was sending people personalized messages about what stocks not to buy, or whether to bring a dog into the family, or whether to date so-and-so, he couldn't carve out a minute to impart the message that a helpless child was being repetitively tortured? This is a tragedy that could have been prevented so easily, if a single believer received a message from God.

So we have another unresolvable paradox in Christianity. Either messages from God are not possible (rendering the

Bible and modern-day Christianity false), or God is choosing not to send messages that can rescue abused children (rendering God cruel and disinterested, not loving and powerful).

There was an infant that died in an apartment not long ago. The parents overdosed on drugs, and left the baby to starve to death over the course of three days. Were there no loving, Christian friends, relatives, even strangers to receive a message from God and rescue this innocent baby? Was the baby being punished for the sins of the father? I am exhausted of excusing God for every unbelievable action *he commits or permits*. A God that allows these things offers me no comfort. It is a consolation to concede that he probably doesn't exist at all. If he does, I can't fathom spending an eternity with a leader who is either that cruel, or that inept.

In my time as a Christian, I listened to 10 years of testimonies to God's great power. Some of the testimonies I heard went like this:

"I had an outdoor birthday party and it rained at my neighbor's house, but not at mine. God is so good."

"I got promoted at work."

"We were able to get that new house."

Even bigger stuff, like:

"I prayed and prayed, and my mother's cancer is cured. All praise to God."

"I was in a terrible accident, and God rescued me from near death."

One testimony that is close to my heart was my own, one I shared in many churches. My home was in foreclosure, and God rescued me. I was able to keep my home, and share this miraculous event with others, as evidence of his great power. I love to hear testimonies. I love that we are able to celebrate amazing, positive things, both big and small, that happen throughout our lives. *But it does beg a couple of questions:*

What about the woman who prayed and prayed, and her mother still died of cancer? What about the child that was kidnapped by a rapist, even though the parents prayed daily for their child's safety? Was God powerful enough to secure my home for me, but powerless to stop another family's three-year-old baby from being stolen by a psychopath? In the accident, what about the other person—the person who died? Sure, God rescued you, but he let someone else die a slow, painful death in the hospital.

Is this a testimony? To what is it a testimony, exactly? To God's sporadic, random power to do great things...sometimes? Or is it (more likely) a testimony of our own ability to affirm the random, positive events that are destined to occur in each of our lives by scientific chance, and to express gratitude when they do?

Many Christians think that terrible events are inevitable, and that they are a sign that the "end times" are nearing. Natural disasters, human tragedies, wars, and diseases are all a sign of God's imminent return to earth. The myth is that everything gets worse with every generation. This thinking is scientifically errant, however.

The flawed concept that "everything is getting worse," has roots in the fact that information and communication improve with each generation. There have always been crimes, and wars, and cruelty, and disease, but we have not always had Twitter to keep us instantly informed. Facebook has not always been there to spread "trending" news to the far corners of the world. The first weekly newspaper was printed in 1605. The earliest newspapers contained around four pages of information, and were distributed only to a few wealthy people. We now have instant access to worldwide news, every hour of every day, right at our fingertips. Even if we don't want it, it comes blasting at us all the time from social media, from a friend's phone, or in closed captions on the TV at the local pub. We see it at the gym, on gas pumps, or every time we search for anything online.

Because of the effort involved to produce and distribute newspapers, in the old days news had to be "newsworthy." Now we can share any shocking or negative piece of information at the click of a button. Whether it is even true is often irrelevant. How many urban legends, posing as warnings, circulate the pages of Facebook? We know about everything terrible, near and far. When someone abuses a pet, or throws a fit at a drive through, or has a scandalous affair, or has a roof blow away in a storm, even on the other side of the world, we know about it. It's no wonder we think the world is worse than ever.

Looking at history objectively, one could argue that the world is, in fact, improving. Diseases that could once wipe out entire populations of people, now have cures. There is a greater awareness regarding spousal and child abuse. There are laws in place, in many countries, that prevent slave labor and child labor. While natural disasters continue, we are ever more equipped to predict them, prepare for them, and save the lives of those affected. Sometimes the same social media that bombards us with news also brings criminals to justice, raises money for disaster victims, and provides resources for anyone who is struggling. To argue that bad things happen to good people because the "Lord is coming soon," is not only very inconsiderate of another's loss, it is also based completely in fantasy and does not at all reflect historical truth. The inherent danger in this line of thinking is, "It's God's will. It's a sign of the times. *So there's nothing we can do about it.*"

The notion of a capricious God, who at any moment might be too busy tending to someone's bank account to protect me from danger, brings me no comfort. In contrast, science is both comforting and empowering. Sure, I'm afraid of being swept away in a tornado or contracting Ebola, but there is a statistically minute chance that either one of these things will happen to me. I know this because the unbiased and non-human God of science consoles me with ratios and percentages, instead of threatening me with curses. If I decide I want further protection, I can educate myself, purchase equipment, or prepare myself physically by relying on scientific sources of information. In this way, I am embracing reality and increasing my odds for success and survival, instead of giving up control and relying on prayers, hope, and the irregular mercy of an unseen power.

Science also offers me the proven hope for eternity. All of the matter inside of us has existed and will exist infinitely, in whatever form it may take: elements, atoms, stars, water, grass, birds. There is no hatred in the God of science. There is only ever-shifting eternity. Constant death, forgiveness of all, and rebirth. A simple, and beautiful design.

Sociopolitical Issues...
sometimes you have to pick sides.

Throughout history, there have been times of peace and prosperity, times not marked by social upheaval, or political unrest. During these times, many choose to remain neutral about politics. But there have been other periods marred by civil unrest, by inequality, poverty, struggle, and fear. In times like these it becomes acutely relevant to choose where you stand. It becomes important to speak out for the oppressed and the marginalized, to stand up for your rights, and to make your voice heard. Many Americans participated in protests during the Emancipation years, the Women's Rights Movement, and the Civil Rights Movement. One quote I saw recently on social media sums it up. "If you are neutral in situations of injustice, you have chosen the side of the oppressor." (Desmond Tutu)

I believe that people will look back on our current time as another period of civil unrest, having a clear-cut definition of who the "good guys" and the "bad guys" were. I'm glad that I can't be counted among those who supported segregation, or those who upheld slavery, or those who denied women equal rights. I certainly don't want to be among those who, now, are doing the same to new groups of people.

Because of the current political climate, I have given higher priority to disassociating with Christianity. I don't want to be mistaken for, nor associated with a group that holds an underlying belief that gays, Muslims, or Jews are going to burn in hell. I don't want any ties to a group that approves of a leader that holds these beliefs. I don't want to be in the same group of people that secretly or openly celebrates the oppression or the trampling of human rights of any group of people. Therefore, if it is necessary to completely sever ties with Christianity, if only to show my love and acceptance to my beautiful, diverse human family, I do so willingly.

————

I absolutely and wholeheartedly stand against the discrimination of any group of people, regardless of race, sexual orientation, gender, or religion. I will not permit my child to be raised in an atmosphere of prejudice of any sort. Not on my watch!

————

Removing Christianity from our lives has opened the possibility to love ourselves and to love and respect others for who they are, without any underlying agenda to change people, judge people, or live apart from people based on how they were born, the belief structure they hold dear, or the life choices they have made. I am now free to instruct my child that all people have inherent worth.

I will always stand on the side of love. Not love and acceptance with an agenda. Real love.

"But most Christians aren't like that," you might say. "Most Christians I associate with are very loving and accepting people."

It's true that many Christians don't hold to fundamentalist, often discriminating views. However, if the underlying doctrine permits prejudice and discrimination, then I can't be for it. I wouldn't join the KKK either, regardless of whether certain sects of the group evolved and became kind and tolerant. Any group that, at its core, practices or preaches exclusivity or discrimination is not the group for me or my family. If only you could see the flamboyant and unrelenting period at the end of that sentence! I refuse to even entertain the ridiculous discussion that "those people" (insert whomever you are bigoted against) are going to hell.

Leaving Christianity publicly clarified my position on discrimination. My association with Christianity seemed to broadcast that I was against certain groups of people. Because Christianity typically stands opposed to gay rights and believes that people of other religions are going to hell, I myself felt oppressed and quieted when it came to vocalizing my beliefs. Today I can stand on my honor, and profess that I am for equality and fair treatment of all individuals. What a beautiful sentiment! Sadly, I anticipate lots of negative feedback from the Christian community, over this one chapter. When I was a Christian, I was told, "You are allowed to love the sinner, as long as you hate their sin."

———————

In other words, to be Christian my heart must be full of love and hatred, in equal proportions.

———————

(I don't have any room in my heart for hating the so-called sins of other people. I'm too busy loving them for who they are, sharing drinks with them by the water, and cracking up as we reminisce about the silly events of our lives. I'm too busy congratulating them on their individual successes, to worry about whether their path lines up with my religious doctrine. I'm also too busy learning about their needs, helping them, and walking beside them, to spend an hour a day praying for them. And I'm a little too honored to be in their presence, to pull out the Bible and tell them all the reasons the Christian God won't accept them into his kingdom. There is no room in my heart for hatred, because it is full of all of these wonderful things.)

But that's just my heart. Each of us can fill our hearts as we choose.

Personal Convictions in Child Rearing...
and it's not even PG-13!

Here's a fun game. The next time you are sharing a well-known Bible story with your children, try stating, in an animated voice, "*Guess what happened next!*" You might want to peek a few verses ahead, before you decide to play this game, because what probably follows this "endearing and uplifting" well-known Bible story is a grisly mass murder. Yep.

Next to the lovely illustration of the walls of Jericho tumbling down, there should be another one of bloody bodies strewn across the ground and over the rubble. There should be one of mothers weeping as they watch their children die, because they were ruthlessly bludgeoned or stoned by "God's people." There should be one of the horrors of corpses burning, while the city is laid to ruin.

After the story of the Ten Commandments, which children so lovingly memorize, "*Guess what happened next!*" Because shortly thereafter, in Exodus 32, we hear God say, "Each of you, take your swords, and go back and forth from one end of the camp to the other. Kill everyone —even your brothers, friends, and neighbors." That day, 3,000 people died. Would that message be confusing to a child, who just learned that one of God's great commandments included not killing? Of course, it's a non-issue because we rarely discuss what happened *next*. It boils down to that nearly magical ability to selectively read the Holy Bible, taking in the little bits of good, and refusing to read, share, talk about, discuss, and question the rest.

It is extremely disturbing to me that children hear, recite, learn and do crafts about stories from the Bible, all the while being gently skirted away from the truth behind each of these stories. The stories are typically about murder, genocide, and a complete lack of disregard for the sanctity of life, all things I would never approve of my child revering. Behind the cutesy little animals of Noah's Ark, lies the almost complete and capricious genocide of the entire human race (if you buy into such an intensely far-fetched story to begin with). Then we have David and Goliath. Here, we boldly share the gruesome end of the tale with our children, and celebrate the killing and *decapitation* of another human being (whether or not he looked different). Later in the story, David is commended for having killed tens of thousands of people. We are teaching our children that the hero kills tens of thousands of people. How is this okay again?

I personally take a stand to teach my child that murder, hate crimes, and "killing for God," are wrong. No matter who did it, regardless of whether they believed "God told them to do it," we are not to revere, respect, honor, or celebrate the killing, harming, hurting of others or destruction of their property. To help teach her this, I have had to suspend letting her participate in Sunday School. It's a choice I'm more than willing to make!

I am also intent on teaching my child to respect the sanctity of all life, including the lives of animals. I don't need much help in this department. In fact, my seven-year-old has taken it upon herself to become a vegetarian, (subject to change, perhaps) and has talked me into doing the same. This was motivated by her love and respect for animals and her distaste for the cruel and abusive practices of today's factory farms. The Bible, contrarily, displays no respect for animal life. Countless animal sacrifices are demanded and recorded throughout the Old Testament. Who can even begin to imagine how many animals have been killed, over thousands of years, because of these twisted, seemingly diabolic requests?

My daughter won't even read *Little House on the Prairie*, and at least in that book they were killing animals to survive. In the Bible animals are slaughtered, without mercy, to bring "gifts" to God. When you think about it, that is cruel, disgusting, and unacceptable. Do you truly think God would create beautiful animal life, and then demand these innocent creatures to be stabbed and burned, their blood strewn over an alter? I'm not picturing a benevolent father, looking down from the clouds. I'm picturing the cover of the creepiest death metal album ever. (No offense, random death metal band!)

Here's what's going on so far. We are busy decriminalizing horrible murders, breezing over genocide to get to the rainbow, and agreeing that animal torture is okay. We're warping our children's minds into believing all of this is fine, why? Because these are the people and creatures God *wants* to kill.

Meanwhile, to shake more confusion into the soup, we are also busy warping things that are a perfectly normal part of human life, such as consensual sex between adults, into something sinful and deserving of hell. I believe these mixed messages are enough to make someone lose their mind. It's no surprise to me that hate crimes, wars, and sexual and emotional abuse often have their root in religion. The Bible is an utter hijacking of human conscience. If you find yourself disagreeing with that statement, then you must think it is worse for a divorced woman to remarry, than it is to slit the throat of your baby pet and spray its blood all over the pulpit. And that makes you…well, weird.

Another parenting concern lies in the Biblical teaching that we are all born wretched sinners and deserving of death. This message runs contradictory to my inherent beliefs and to a core message I continually impart to my child. All human beings have inherent worth. We are not meaningless, or dispensable. Babies are born innocent, and have the basic human right to make their own life choices as they grown into adults, as long as they are not causing intentional harm to others.

I believe my daughter to be a precious, invaluable work of art. A shining star in the universe. I would be devastated if my child internalized the message that she was worthless, or deserving of hell. I would consider it a great failure on my part, as a parent, if she did. And yet, this emotionally disturbing message is imparted to Christian children through use of color boards, before they can even read or reason for themselves! It is imparted almost every week thereafter, until the child cannot unlearn it. I'm sure it's not at all traumatizing to explain to a three-year old that they were so full of black sin that someone had to shed their red blood and take their own life, so that they could be white as snow and forgiven. I say that, of course, seeping with sarcasm, but many Christians churches would argue that it is, in fact, a wonderful message to share with their toddlers.

I will never forget the dinner discussion in which my (then) little six-year-old told me the story about how she deserved to go to hell, just for being born. She was taught this terribly sad and untrue concept at one of her favorite places. And here you have it. My one "Christian sorrow" that I will carry with me forever, having exposed her to that very horrible and demoralizing message. Though I recognize that those who taught her this had hearts full of good intentions, the message cannot be construed any other way than a very haunting idea of worthlessness. I was warned by several intelligent people that my daughter would hear this if I raised her in church. I wish I had listened. I cannot undo it. I can only hope that a child who figured out the Santa Claus myth at four, will be smart enough to see this for what it is. Foolish lies. But foolish lies can be damaging to the heart, the mind, and the soul, when you are six.

Going back to confusing messages, the Christian vilification of sex is terribly damaging. Healthy, consensual sex between single adults should not ever be restricted by any government or religious entity. As sex has been proven to be one of the basic human needs[10], inflicting what amounts to emotional abuse for something completely normal has led to, at a minimum, many people's discomfort and stress. At worst, it has led to pedophilia, or other forms of sexual perversion.[11]

I intend to raise my child with a healthy mentality towards human sexuality, and her own growth and development. It would be horrible if religious beliefs caused her to blame herself for absolutely normal thoughts and feelings as she grows and matures. It would also be unacceptable, to me, to raise her in an atmosphere that condemns others for theirs. As I mentioned previously, children have committed suicide because they can't live up to their religious parents' expectations, or because they have heard a bullying message from their peers (even their well-intentioned Christian peers) or they have discovered they are gay and believe they're going to hell. *Why would I want to take even the smallest chance of this happening to my child?*

No child should have to live, much less die wondering if they are going to hell. I view that like raising your child in a nightmare from which they can't awaken.

Additionally, my child's body is hers. I consider it borderline abusive to instruct her on what she can and can't do with it. I do not own her. My job is to give her the confidence and the resources to make wise decisions on her own, as she matures. I strongly refuse to impart the message that "Biblical marriage" as it's called, is the only appropriate place for sex to happen. Has anyone read the examples painted for us of "Biblical marriage" in the actual Bible? All I see is polygamy, rape, and concubines. In fact, lying down with a woman (even taken against her will) defined marriage in parts of the Old Testament. I'm not sure how or when it was decided that a "Biblical marriage" was the morally appropriate one.

Here's a hard reality. We don't get to pick who our children become. Yes, we can influence their self-esteem, their knowledge base, their access to appropriate entertainment, their level of physical activity, their diet. What we don't get to do is decide what they're going to like, who they're going to fall in love with, what career they'll pursue, what gender they'll be attracted to. And even if we force them into decisions we approve of, anything from what they wear, to what they believe (and I hope we don't do this) we are not actually making them like these things, we're only forcing them to pretend to be somebody they're not. In my personal experience, this can lead to a sense of worthlessness, and can cause depression. Inevitably, when our children are grown, we will lose the power to control their choices. They will find their own identity.

Hopefully, we have been there all along, allowing them to grow into the person they truly are, and not missing out on knowing that person. I don't want to know a child that I've created in my imagination, and miss out on the once-in-a-lifetime chance to know and love my real child as she grows. I'm in amazed by who she is! Even so young, I have learned from her, everything from bizarre factoids, to important views on life, animals, the earth. The last thing I would ever want would be for this beautiful child to be waiting by the door, anxious to leave an overbearing and manipulative mother, as soon as it becomes legal to do so. Nor do I want to waste my valuable energy trying to change another human being. Human beings have inherent rights. Children are human beings. That means my child has rights.

And so do yours.

An extremely detrimental message in the Bible is that women and girls are less clean and more sinful than men. (I Timothy 2:11, Leviticus 12:1-5, Numbers 5:15-31, Ecclesiastes 7:28) Women are also expected to be subservient to men. I have attended countless church services that strive to downplay or explain away this teaching and adapt it to more modern viewpoints. Nevertheless, the Biblical stance on women's subservience is clear. (I Corinthians 11:3, I Timothy 2:11-14, Titus 2:3-5, Genesis 3:16, Ephesians 5:23) I will not allow my daughter to be infused with the message that she is intrinsically less capable or valuable than her male counterparts. If I had a boy, I would be just as adamant about teaching him that all people are equal. And if there really were a God that sent an entire book to Earth for us to read and learn from, I believe he would have gone out of his way to impart the scientific truth that menstrual periods do not make those around you unclean (see below, for the Biblical view of menstruation), and girls are every bit as valuable as boys, and other such obvious truths.

"When a woman has a discharge, and the discharge in her body is blood, she shall be in her menstrual impurity for seven days, and whoever touches her shall be unclean until the evening. And everything on which she lies during her menstrual impurity shall be unclean. Everything also on which she sits shall be unclean. And whoever touches her bed shall wash his clothes and bathe himself in water and be unclean until the evening. And whoever touches anything on which she sits shall wash his clothes and bathe himself in water and be unclean until the evening. Whether it is the bed or anything on which she sits, when he touches it he shall be unclean until the evening...(Leviticus 15:19-30) **[Says the unchanging, infallible word of God]**

If a man lies with a woman during her menstrual period and uncovers her nakedness, he has made naked her fountain, and she has uncovered the fountain of her blood. Both of them shall be cut off from among their people. (Leviticus 20:18) **[Time to start getting rid of—probably all grownups.]**

Let a woman learn quietly with all submissiveness. I do not permit a woman to teach or to exercise authority over a man; rather, she is to remain quiet. For Adam was formed first, then Eve; and Adam was not deceived, but the woman was deceived and became a transgressor. Yet she will be saved through childbearing—if they continue in faith and love and holiness, with self-control. (1 Timothy 2:11-15) **[It's pretty scary that this is still being taught. A woman is an unworthy sinner that needs to shut up and obey. Her only worth is being able to conceive and bear children.]**

As for my child's education, why would I teach her ancient myths, many of them tribal in nature, that completely conflict with science and proven facts? There are some truths to be found in the Bible, when interpreted as parables, and positive messages can be extracted from it. (Though I would argue that one could extract a positive message from absolutely anything, any book, any song, any work of art. If one can see through the Bible's endless spew of horror stories and extract positive messages from them, one could presumably do the same with true stories from history, incredible works of fiction, or even the *Nightmare on Elm Street* films.) But if the stories of creation, Noah's Ark, etc. are expected to be taken literally, then I would have to stretch my imagination to the degree of believing that this entire life and the history of mankind as we know it is all an illusion.

It has been over a year since my (then) six-year-old began to challenge Bible stories at the dinner table, with her knowledge of scientific facts and even with philosophy. She would often come home perplexed by the stories taught in Sunday school, as she couldn't reconcile them with science and history as she understood it. "How could God's entire plan be destroyed by one person eating a piece of fruit? If he had a perfect plan, why would he even create that fruit?" "If we're just now receiving light from galaxies that have been gone for millions of years, how can the earth have been created on the same day as the heavens?"

At the dinner table recently, I asked her what her take on the Noah's Ark story was. Her reply?

> God pretty much killed everybody in the entire Earth, except one family and two of every animal. Then he put a little rainbow in the sky and basically said, "It's okay. I didn't do anything bad *to you*, and that's all that matters. Nothing bad happened here!"

She then preceded to ask me questions like, "Did God only have it out for the mammals? What about the fish? They didn't die." That made me think of how absurdly overpopulated the earth would have been with fish and sea creatures, and maybe birds and insects, while only a few mammals roamed. Then she asked, "What about whales? What about creatures that can live in and outside of the water? What about the walking catfish?" (At that, I laughed, because I was certain that had to be the name of a jazz band or something, and that she had mistaken it for an actual fish. Turns out... it's a real thing.)

At any rate, it may seem silly to even dedicate half a page to absurdities so obvious that a seven-year-old can't miss them. And yet, many people alive today believe that the story of Noah's Ark happened, line for line, as written in the Bible, and not that it is a deluge myth similar to those that appear in over 30 ancient cultures and religions. (Check out Wikipedia's extensive list on the cultures with deluge myths.[12]) I'm all for a good story, and I can appreciate the art and culture, the history that shines through these ancient tales. But can I realistically cling to a tribal explanation of nature and science, in the year 2017?

He is the King of Kings, Lord of Lords, Prince of Princes, the Governor of the World. He traveled to far lands, teaching goodness, and piercing all darkness with his light. He suffered and died, was laid under a shroud, and buried in a tomb. But to the great rejoicing of all, he rose again to everlasting life! The tomb was empty! We know he is not just a myth, but a true person who walked the earth, because of how many eye witnesses there are to the story. In fact, for thousands of years, people still celebrated his birth in the Holy Land, by lighting candles and singing songs.

Jesus?

Nope! Osiris. The above is taken from ancient Greek writings dated 1570-1070 BCE.[13]

I personally devoted way too much effort to reconciling Biblical myths with science, during my time as a Christian. If to follow a religious dogma you must shelve the composite of acquired human knowledge and your own discernment of the obviously fantastical, it is a dangerous dogma and should be viewed with distrust, if considered at all. The Bible does in fact encourage **not** to discern, **not** to reason, **not** to seek truth. (Proverbs 3:5, Proverbs 3:7, James 1:5-8, Psalms 119:66, 1Corinthians 3:18) At church we are taught to suspend our own reasoning, to trust that God has a purpose for everything.

Conversely, I would encourage my child to question everything! Have a healthy respect for the unknown, and for others' opinions of what the unknown might represent. The quest for knowledge and understanding should never be subdued. It's logical to believe that if something is true, other writings and events will corroborate it, and attempts to debunk it will fail. Ever wonder why fossils billions of years old have been unearthed and dated by scientists, yet no one can find any solid physical evidence of Biblical events that occurred a few thousand years ago, with the exception of the Bible itself? Sounds a little fishy to me. Suppose the roles were reversed, and scientists found an old book that described the scientific creation of the universe, the big bang, single-cell lifeforms, the existence of gigantic creatures that ruled the earth. Now imagine that no subsequent physical evidence was ever discovered to back up that story, no bone unearthed, no trace of early lifeforms, no footprints, or DNA, or patterns in the universe that would suggest there was a shred of truth to that scientific book. Would we jump to the conclusion that the book was true, and teach billions of children worldwide to believe in it and conclude that every other conflicting piece of evidence was clearly false, because it ran counter to what the "book" said? Would we tell them, "You are not allowed to question this?" Would we threaten them with an eternal time out, when they did?

> *If you left your life and followed him, you would be part of his eternal family. He would be your father, your defender. If you were poor, weak, marginalized, he would offer you hope. He would fight for the rights of the misunderstood. He would allow you free will, but truly didn't want you to leave his fold. He would test the faith of his followers. They needed to love him more than they loved their own lives. It didn't matter why. It was their job to trust, to have faith like a child.*

Jesus?

Nope. Jim Jones, who organized a mass suicide, and killed more than 900 people, in the name of his "religion."[14]

'If any of you come to me,' he said to them, *'and don't hate your father and your mother, your wife and your children, your brothers and your sisters – yes, and even your own life! – you can't be my disciple.'*

Jim Jones?

Nope. Jesus. (Luke 14:26)

But isn't it still better to raise kids in a contemporary Christian church, even if we don't *really believe everything,* **since it will enhance their childhood and encourage them to make healthy life choices?**

I'm glad you asked! Before you're tempted (as I was) to think that churchgoing is somehow equated with "a better life," let's look at the statistics.

1. Divorce rates among Christians are significantly higher than other faith groups, and much higher than atheists and agnostics.[15]

2. Teen pregnancy is higher in conservative religious states.[16]

3. 45% of Christians admit that pornography is a problem in their home. 54% of pastors admit to having viewed porn recently. (To ensure I'm not being biased, I'm taking this one from a Christian poll.)[17]

4. Religious individuals are up to three times as likely to suffer from depression than non-religious.[18]

5. This study shows that Christian children are less empathetic and less altruistic than their non-religious counterparts.[19]

6. Domestic violence against women is at least as prevalent in Christian homes as in non-religious ones. But because of Christian views, wives are often encouraged to continue in the marriage, putting them at greater risk than their non-religious counterparts. (This is taken from a Christian study.)[20]

7. Religious children are less able to distinguish fantasy from reality.[21] (call me not surprised.)

Intermission...

"He Hath a Blemish"

God was on his third Cuban coffee, pounding through the Book of Leviticus. After all, it was 500 BC. Time was running out to finish the Old Testament, and he was only a few chapters in. "Let's see," thought God. "Who's cool enough to approach my holy temple?" There were a few people that just wouldn't do. Those guys, oh, and those guys. God scribbled and tossed, scribbled and tossed, his pen smoking. Moses caught the notes, as they fell through the smoky clouds. Upon reading, he shook his head and blamed the coffee. But what could he do?

Speak unto Aaron, saying, Whosoever he be of thy seed in their generations that hath any blemish, let him not approach to offer the bread of his God.

For whatsoever man he be that hath a blemish, he shall not approach: a blind man, or a lame, or he that hath a flat nose, or any thing superfluous,

Or a man that is brokenfooted, or brokenhanded,

Or crookbackt, or a dwarf, or that hath a blemish in his eye, or be scurvy, or scabbed, or hath his stones broken;

No man that hath a blemish of the seed of Aaron the priest shall come nigh to offer the offerings of the LORD made by fire: he hath a blemish; he shall not come nigh to offer the bread of his God.

Historical and Societal Concerns...
Christianity's infamous legacy, then and now.

Yes, the verse we enjoyed in our intermission is indeed from the Bible. And while I've had a few chuckles at its expense, there is also a darker side to the prejudice portrayed therein. It is religious belief that often marginalizes anyone who is "different." Even in 2017, with all of the advantages of modern science, medicine, and legal defense, we are still allowing religion to dictate who is "normal" and who is "unworthy." Who can imagine the quantity of massacres, beatings, oppression, prejudice, and cruelty to people and animals, committed in the name of religion before we had these things?

Even if we disregard all of the atrocities committed by God's people in the Bible as fiction, the number of true ones recorded in history is stunning. Just to name a few off the top of my head, there is the Inquisition, the Crusades, the Catholic-Protestant wars of Ireland, the Thirty Years' War, the Ottoman Conquests, Nazi concentration camps, the African slave trade, the oppression and slaughter of tribal people, the persecution of pagans, violence against and oppression of women, and currently, hate crimes and killings of Muslims, Jews, and gay people. If you're

interested, a quick Google search will pull up hundreds of tragedies, ranging from individual cases of abuse, to full-on genocide, all in the name of God.

No religion is exempt from these atrocities. Christians like to
think of themselves as the "true" religion, citing the terrorist
attacks committed by Islamic extremists. In fact, Christians
and Muslims are at least head-to-head in wars, massacres, and
crimes against humanity. Some statistics put Christianity way
ahead of Islam, when it comes to violence and killing.[22] In looking at the damage caused by religion, we can't only look at the
last 50 years. Religions seem to take turns being the oppressor
and the oppressed, the "good guys," and the "bad guys." It might
not be "our turn," in grand scale, at this precise moment in history. However, there are many current examples of Christian
terrorism, even in the United States. [23]

If we look at the collective damage of religions, all religions,
it becomes apparent that our world would be better off without it. Every group thinks the other group is going to hell.
Therefore, "those people" are not as important. It doesn't
matter if we trample their rights, force them to agree with
us, murder them. We are so busy arguing over the semantics
of what "being good" means, that we are not being good to
each other at all. If we could just "zoom out" for a second and
realize that the Christian religion is part of this, maybe we
could see how silly it is. We think they're going to hell. They
think we're going to hell. The other guy thinks this other guy

is going to hell. Come on. Really? I know first-graders with a more mature approach to life than this. Meanwhile every day, every year, every decade, every century, we miss out on the opportunity to share this Earth peacefully with one another. To lift each other up. To impact our place and time in history with kindness, and empathy.

An estimated 50,000 women and men were killed by Christians for the crime of "Witchcraft" between 1560 and 1693. (A very conservative estimate)[24]

"Sometimes the Scripture declareth that women and children must perish with their parents. Sometimes the case alters, but we will not dispute it now. We have sufficient light from the Word of God for our proceedings." (Captain John Underhill, after the Christian slaughter of Pequot Indians, 1637)[25]

Eric Rudolph, of the Army of God, bombed Centennial Park, during the Summer Olympics of 1996, an abortion clinic, in 1998, and a lesbian bar, in 1997. The Army of God supported his actions. [26]

In 2012, Gateway Christian Military Academy, in Florida, beat and berated helpless children, in the name of "God," to correct their behavior. Children were subject to ridicule and bloodied, bruised, choked, tortured, confined to seclusion, and beaten to near loss of life. And yet, religious exemptions allowed these homes to avoid state restrictions on corporal punishment. These homes were supported, perforce, by unwitting tax payers in the community. [27]

With encouragement from the Russian Orthodox Church, Vladimir Putin is currently passing laws that violate the human rights of the LGBT community. The laws affect the adoption of children by gay couples, and permit the jailing of anyone (even tourists) suspected of being gay. He is in the process of considering a law that could remove children from their parents, if the parents are even suspected of being homosexual. During a peaceful protest of these of these heinous laws, hundreds of Orthodox Christians attacked and beat the protesters. This is happening now, in 2017.[28]

This is not to say that there aren't millions of wonderful and kind religious people. Unfortunately, at its core religion is about politics, power, and money, all dressed up as the "loving worship of supreme beings and hope for eternal life." How much can we justify, get away with, or gain in the name of our god? How many lands can we conquer? How many slaves can we take? How many walls can we build, to separate "us" from "them?" Like a corporation with good employees but evil management, Christianity (as well as other religions) "employs" well-meaning and sincere believers, faithful and hopeful, many of whom were raised to believe that any information that doesn't line up with the Bible is a lie. Meanwhile "upper management" perpetrates prejudice and oppression, covers criminal behavior, stalls progress in science and medicine, and tramples the rights of anyone "different," even using the loyalty, dedication, and funds of its members to do so.

In addition to perpetuating problems in society, Christianity also has a secondary detrimental effect on society. Most of the believers are focused on the afterlife, and not on actual life—the planet itself and they people they share the planet with now. There is little focus on protecting our precious planet because of the prevailing notion that this world will pass away as part of God's plan. It is scientifically documented that the Earth is polluted and in distress, and that changes need to be made if we are to survive as a race, but scientific evidence is blatantly ignored by Christians when it doesn't "fit" the Christian theory. In addition, there is little emphasis on bettering one's own physical, emotional, or financial state, since suffering, poverty, humility, and weakness are favored in the teachings of Jesus. Persecution is ignored, unless it is against Christians. Serious ecological damage and harm to animals is disregarded, while church members place all of their focus on the imagined concerns of the apocalypse, the rapture, and converting nonbelievers.

The collective "people-power" of churchgoers is impressive. There are over 326 million people living in this country. Of them, an estimated 20 percent attend church weekly. In the United States alone, we are talking about *64 million people* who regularly give of their time and money to "God's work." If their dedication were redirected into something truly beneficial to human life, I can only imagine the exponential improvement in every cause that's plaguing our planet. With the power of 64 million people who are working weekly to affect change, we could stamp out abuse, feed the world, clean up the atmosphere, and control animal endangerment. We could get foster kids into families, grow food that isn't toxic, build tiny homes for the homeless, and collect enough money to buy toys, books, and clothes for families that truly need them.

So many opportunities to love others, love our planet, love our animals, and love ourselves are discarded in favor of church attendance, Bible reading, evangelizing, criticizing, judging, and collecting money so that our church can have the hippest coffee bar and the coolest stage lighting.

I am not underestimating the charitable efforts of churches around the world. I have read reports that identify religious individuals as the mostly likely to give to charitable efforts. However, I'd like to explore why the statistics may be skewed when it comes to religion and giving. First of all, most of America's charitable giving goes to the religious institutions themselves. This amounted to $122.94 billion dollars, in 2016.[29]

———

This form of "religious charity" represented by self-serving gifts to the church, seems more like a membership fee than anything remotely altruistic.

———

Churches are rich and have the means to tabulate giving. Statements are issued, and finances are tracked by church staff. Smaller groups, like atheists and agnostics, give of what they have without the paperwork, since there is rarely a large organization backing their efforts or tracking their finances.

Furthermore, it would be impossible to define, much less calculate the daily charitable efforts of individuals worldwide. A school employee who purchases a lunch for a child with no money. A police officer who looks the other way, instead of removing a homeless person from a warm, but illegal shelter. A son who moves in with his elderly mother, to help pay the bills. A caring stranger who donates blood after a tragedy, or another who tosses coins in the hat of a subway musician. True charity is the one that no one is tracking.

When charitable gifts are given to large Christian organizations, inevitably a portion of the funds is separated out and dedicated to proselytizing, reducing the percentage of funds that will be applied to the problem. Yes, you may be feeding a hungry child or sending Christmas gifts to impoverished children, but a portion of your gift will also go to teaching kids about Jesus, or purchasing Bibles, or planting a church, or attempting to convert people, or abolish their traditional beliefs and practices. I'm sure that is a plus to most Christians, as they believe that is the most valuable work they can accomplish. I am only clarifying that when it comes to running numbers, nonreligious charities are not removing a percentage of the charitable donation, to redirect it towards separate ulterior motives for personal gain. If a religious charity collects a million dollars, and 10% of it is applied to evangelizing, then $100 thousand has gone right back into the Christian church.

Another reason statistics are skewed in favor of religious charity is that churches often have the financial means and the people power to create and promote large charities. This facilitates giving through "religious" relief efforts. It does not mean that there aren't many wonderful charities that are non-religious in nature. It only means that the religious ones have a greater presence on street corners, in television ads, and in social media. This is simply because they have the funds to create this presence.

I would argue that all Christian giving is ultimately self-serving. Help is offered to the needy and marginalized only when that help comes with the ulterior motive of "reaching people for Jesus." Genuinely loving and giving to others, with absolutely no desire to change their belief system or lifestyle, provides an impactful gift to both the giver and the receiver. However, if there is an underlying motive such as recruiting another person into a belief, both parties suffer. On part of the Christian, all the good done to another would be considered a failure if that person failed to accept Jesus in the end. The receiver also suffers, because the gift they received is viewed as a sales pitch, and not unconditional love. "I know that you brought me this food because you want me to accept your god, not because I'm hungry." This can leave a sense of belittlement, instead of empowerment.

It's a lot like getting a birthday card from a car dealership. We open them and toss them in the garbage. We don't have the sensation, even for a minute, that that salesperson truly thought of us on our birthday. It's about the sale. Another illustration of this would be a husband that displays love for his wife or remains faithful because he believes God commands it, and not because he genuinely feels it. At what point does "living for God," rob the world around you of your genuine care?

I read that the tax-exempt state of churches costs our country an astonishing $71 billion dollars a year![30] I know that the implications of taxing a religious organization are complex, and there's a better space for a heated debate than this short chapter of a book. But here's some food for thought. You and I pay out of pocket, to make up for the tax exemptions churches enjoy. Why? Because government programs must be funded from taxes. We cover every single religious organization with our hard-earned money, including the Church of Scientology, lavishly wealthy megachurches, and cults. Remember Jim Jones, from a few pages back? His cult, People's Temple, was tax exempt thanks to laws that protect religious organizations from taxation. The abduction, abuse, and murder that occurred in his organization was subsidized by all Americans, regardless of their religious standing. Here's another factoid. The cost of food stamps for the entire fiscal year of 2016 was $70.9 billion[31] less than the amount churches would provide to our country in one year, if they were taxed. Doesn't that put the whole conservative argument against welfare in a brand new light? If churches weren't getting away with these incredible tax breaks, we could afford to feed every poor person in this country, year after year, at no extra cost.

That fact led me to muse about the sad condition of our society: homelessness, cuts in school programs, minimum wage payments that have inched up only a dollar a decade, poverty, hunger, foreclosures. The very people who claim to be the workers of good in society are wrapping their time and financial resources back into the "church entity." They are not just missing out on, but preventing a tangible impact on society. Can you imagine if believers, instead of closing themselves in a building for two hours a week, went out and helped a living person who is suffering for those same two hours a week? Can you imagine if the ten percent tithe, or the financial gift of any amount, were given directly to a family in need? Can you imagine if churches, like any other big corporation, were taxed? If the billions of dollars and millions of hours given to God were invested in our country, where could this nation be today?

Let's set aside the tax argument for a moment. I know that churches do good, and many charities are funded by Christians. However, a large portion of the funds are undeniably self-serving, with explicit use for Christians and the members of the church and their families. If you like road trips as much as I do, you might be able to prove this point for yourself. On our last road trip across the country, my daughter and I took note that even in terribly impoverished small towns there was always at least one gleaming, state-of-the-art church. Yes, some money goes to charity, but it is evident that funds also go into lavish church structures and amenities. Again, all Christian charity is self-serving on some level, as the charitable work is decidedly purposed to recruit new Christians.

Aside from the direct havoc religion wreaks on society in the form of killing, hating, or neglecting to help others, it also effects the enjoyment of the arts and pop culture. Many Christians restrict themselves from poetry, music, movies, and all forms of art that do not comply with Christian morality. This robs Christians of the inspiration and the education that comes from observing life's diversity. In short, everything is filtered through the narrow lens of Christianity. Every observation must be checked for compliance to this strict moral code. Christians I have spoken with often find themselves unsure as to whether they should "allow themselves" to watch certain shows, listen to certain songs, or read certain books. They are unable to feel genuine, unadulterated excitement to partake with and learn from others along the life journey because they feel pressured to constantly gauge the "holiness" of every interaction. In some cases, Christians push for censorship beyond their immediate circle and onto society as well. If something is not "God honoring," (whatever that might mean, at any given time to one Christian church or another) then it should be banned, censored, or burned.

After a long and bloody combat, Christianity, aided by a host of miracles and the burning sincerity of its adherents, defeated and wiped out the old faith of the pagans. Then with great fervor and diligence, it strove to cast out and utterly destroy every least possible occasion of sin; and in doing so, it ruined or demolished all of the marvelous statues, besides the other sculptures, the pictures, mosaics and ornaments representing false pagan gods; and as well as this, it destroyed countless memorials and inscriptions left in honor of illustrious persons who had been commemorated by the genius of

*the ancient world, in statues and other public adornments...
their tremendous zeal was responsible for inflicting severe
damage on the practice of the arts, which then fell into total
confusion.* (Georgio Vasari)

1600's: Christmas celebrations are banned in America,
by Puritans.[32]

Late-1800s: The Southern Baptist town of Elmore,
Oklahoma bans dancing. The ban lasts until 1980, and
its lift inspires the movie *Footloose.*[33]

1956-1957: Several reverends and Catholic priests speak
out against Elvis Presley, and warn their church members not to attend his concerts.[34]

1961: Landmark cases rule blue laws constitutional,
restricting commercial activities (particularly the purchase of alcohol) on Sunday, in many states. Blue laws
exist to honor the Sabbath, or a Biblical day of rest.[35]

1930-2008: Playing football on Sunday is banned in
Protestant Northern Ireland, to observe the Sabbath.[36]

2000-2007: Many Christian denominations fight to ban
Harry Potter books, stating they "normalize magic" and
are occult in nature.[37]

2009: Amazing Grace Baptist Church destroys Bibles that are not King James Version, as well as works by Christian authors that they disagree with.[38]

2017: A Christian-run cinema bans the showing of *Beauty and the Beast* for having a gay character.[39]

These are just some (ridiculous, but true!) examples of how the Christian agenda has permeated every facet of art and entertainment, for hundreds of years.

A common sentiment among Christians is the desire to live "apart" from the world. This manifests in varied ways, from refusing to acknowledge the inherent value of different religions and belief systems, to homeschooling children so they won't be exposed to lessons that contradict the creation myth and other Christian beliefs, to buying computer programs that "wash" movies and other works of art of any material Christian may find offensive, to refusing self-education on current human affairs, to a general preference of convening only with like-minded individuals. During my long escape from Christianity, I wrestled with the perceived benefit of "sheltering" my child from many of the difficult truths in the world. Censoring and carefully selecting what she was exposed to did have its lure. After all, who really wants their first grader to understand the lyrics to most songs on the radio, or to have full access to an unsupervised YouTube vortex? Keeping her from almost everything, in the name of religion, was an easy, blanket remedy for not making difficult parenting decisions. I often asked myself the question, "Do I really want my child to grow up in this crazy, messed up world?

Well, guess what? This IS the world. It may not be perfect, but it's the only one we have. And yes! I want my child to live, to love, to grow, to learn, and to be in this world. I want her to bear both the joys and the burdens of her contemporaries. I want her to feel the complexity of truth, the glory and the angst of art, the unshaken acceptance of reality, the awe of the unknown. I don't want to rob her of this world, this time, her time! I want every moment to matter, to be tangibly and poignantly real, unwashed, with no walls around us.

The Negative Impact of Prayer...
try this at home!

I will irrefutably prove that prayer is ineffective, in one paragraph:

Jesus states "If ye shall ask anything in my name, I will do it." (John 14:14) A one-minute experiment will prove this false. You can try it at home! Go outside and pray for something random to fall from the sky. Please contact me if your request is granted. For the purpose of this paragraph, I'll assume it was not. Christians explain away this verse and other teachings about prayer like this. "God always answers prayer. What you need to understand is that God's answer isn't always yes. Sometimes it's no. Sometimes it's not now." Well, common sense will tell you that these are the same exact odds as leaving things to chance! If you are praying for someone to get a new job, God's answer will be yes, no, or maybe someday. Likewise, if this person simply applies for a job and you don't pray for them, they will get it, not get it, or maybe get it someday. There is a 0-degree difference in the results with or without prayer, *even by Christian standards.* This renders prayer completely ineffective, outside of providing a false sense of having helped someone.

Not to mention, there have been scientific studies on this.[40]

But surely it can't hurt to pray, can it? Ah, prayer. It's so easy, and free to give anyone who asks for it. But we've just shown that prayer helps zero percent of the time, and is the same as leaving things to chance. Guess what helps someone 100 percent of the time? *Actually helping them.* This brings me to the negative impact of prayer.

Here's another experiment you can conduct at home. Start a prayer chain, verbally, or on social media. It can go something like this. "Prayer request. I need help with [insert something real here.] I can use all the prayer I can get." Then tally up how many people respond with "Praying!" and how many respond with a tangible offer of help, which you cleverly also asked for.

I wish I could go back and take away every time I responded to such a request with, "I'm praying for you!" It's oh-so-easy to type. Praying enabled me to check that little box in my heart, the one that makes me feel like I did something good, something helpful. Had I not placed faith in something useless, I might have opted to do something impactful.

In my opinion, prayer becomes a negative force when it is used in place of anything that can verifiably change the situation. In the Christian community, it's common to pray for a sick friend instead of offering to cook for her, pick up her child from school, search for an online home remedy, or drive her to the doctor. Positive action is replaced with a useless gesture. The general sentiment is that something has been done to help, when in fact nothing has been done to help. On a large scale, the world is negatively impacted when people choose to pray for the homeless, victims of natural disasters, starving children, addicts, or survivors of abuse, instead of offering more effective forms of assistance. The people who are inclined to help would likely offer genuine assistance, if they didn't feel they were already helping by sending prayers.

A scientific look at cause marketing provides a clear example of how "feeling we are helping" can backfire. Cause marketing is the current trend to attach a cause to a product, a prevalent example being the pink-labeled products during breast cancer awareness month. Research has shown that people would prefer to purchase a product with a pink label, than one without it.[41] They already planned to purchase that yogurt or that box of cereal, so it's an easy decision. They don't actually have to "give" any more money than they'd already expected to spend, but they're still awarded with the sensation that they did something altruistic. Consumers who buy cause marketing products end up giving less to social causes or charities.[42] Why? Because they have been led to believe that they already did their part to help.

The irony is, a cause label is no guarantee that any money from the purchase will go towards any charity.[43] Any company can put an awareness label on their product. It doesn't necessarily indicate that a percentage of the sale goes toward the cause. Companies that do contribute often have caps on the amount they will donate, and there is no way of knowing if this cap has already been met. They may continue selling products with the cause label and the promise of a donation, even after the cap has been reached. Furthermore, the products themselves may contain ingredients or toxins that *negatively* impact the cause! Think Before You Pink, a project of Breast Cancer Action hosts several campaigns to raise awareness about the dangers of cause marketing in the breast cancer community.[44]

———

Misguided altruism, especially in large scale, causes more harm than good. Prayer is misguided altruism.

———

The Tithe...
the financial burden of being Christian

Now we've come to that 10 percent of your income, which you're supposed to give to God.

I continue to be a proponent of giving. Giving is good when it is voluntary, and not expected or elicited. I will also preface the following by stating that I was never forced or coerced to give a tithe by any pastor or leader of a church. However, I always gave my tithe not out of a desire to give, but out of a desire to obey God. I had plenty of other arenas in which I truly desired to give, but I had to refrain, in order to fulfill my duty of giving to the church. To be fair, I did enjoy the benefits provided me by the collective tithe, free coffee and snacks at church, the heat, the air conditioning, and the occasional family outing. But while I spent years sacrificially giving of my finances, I never got to see a smile on a friend's face when I rescued them from some financial worry. I never felt the joy of bailing my sister out of a debt, or helping my dad into a better car, or blessing a stranger on the street with a hundred-dollar bill. Every single time I gave, over the course of those 10 years, my gift got sucked into the netherworld of church bureaucracy. I got a quarterly receipt for it and the sensation that I had complied with some Christian duty.

Everything I gave, I did so voluntarily. Though it could be argued that a repeated message/threat is a form of coercion, I don't even believe the churches themselves expected it of me. Most pastors I have known on a more personal level have confessed that they are uncomfortable instructing on giving, but they believe God commands it of them so that the church members will not lose the blessings that come from tithing. However it materialized, I definitely felt a strong "spiritual" pressure to give a tithe, and I was completely convinced that if I did not, I was "robbing God," and that financial problems would befall me.

The first year after my husband left me a single mother with a toddler, I faced literal hunger. I was unable to work the hours that I had before becoming a mom, and on top of it I had another mouth to feed. Yet even in those darkest days of financial strain and worry, I still felt compelled to write the church a check, if only for $10. Several times I bounced those checks, putting myself into financial devastation for the month, as the bank would charge me a fee, which resulted in another fee, etc. Looking back, I can see that I put my own daughter in harm's way, financially speaking, in the name of obedience to the God I feared. And when I chose not to give, (because I truly couldn't afford it) I felt sad, and ashamed, and unworthy.

There are some very telling reports online about the billions of dollars that trickle into churches annually.[45] It's particularly disturbing in demographics that tend to face financial hardship. [46]

It's chilling to read online articles about the billions of dollars African American churches have earned, while little or none of the money seems to be trickling back and supporting the individuals in the community. I also found several articles about lower-income families, across races, who have expressed such dedication to the tithe that they are willing to lose their homes before they cease giving to the church. I read many personal stories of good, trusting people who continued to give, through sickness and poverty, only to later conclude that the church was prospering off their sacrifice. I decided against providing direct links to these personal stories in my own book, but I would highly encourage you to do a Google search on how tithing affects lower-income families in the United States and the world.

I remember being morally perplexed during the time I was receiving food stamps. Was it unsavory, or maybe even illegal for me to be giving away my money when the government was paying for my food? Would I face repercussion from the government if I did tithe, or from God if I did not? I spent hours online, trying to determine if I could lose my benefits if my tithing were discovered by the government. Eventually, it didn't sit well in my soul to give away money when my basic needs were being met by public assistance, presumably so that I could have some leftover cash to pay bills and transportation and to meet my daughter's clothing and schooling needs. I ceased paying the tithe, but still gave offerings whenever I believed God was pressuring me to do so.

I am still a giver. The difference is, I now understand the true purpose of giving. It is not to suffer, or strangle yourself financially to prove your faith. It also shouldn't become so routine that it is considered a bill, another regular monthly debt. Giving should induce joy. It should involve sporadically and *freely* sharing money or time with someone in need. It is to bless someone with a surprise. It is to step outside of your comfort zone and anonymously send someone a care package, not because you want them to convert to your religion, but because they are a human being, and so are you. It is to send a gift to a total stranger, somewhere across the world. It is not about a forced, calculated percentage. It is ultimately about love.

I sent a gift to a child I will never meet, through Travelling Tutus. Travelling Tutus is one of a few awesome organizations that collect dance costumes and send them to needy families around the world. Dresses for dance recitals are expensive, and they are usually only used once or twice, for a few minutes. How amazing to imagine that some lovely girl in Pakistan, or Africa, or Guatemala has danced in the dress my daughter wore. It brings my heart joy to think that I had some part in making a child's dream a reality. I mention this only to demonstrate that giving doesn't require a strenuous financial sacrifice. It just requires a thoughtful search for ways to bless others with what you already have. It may require loving beyond the front door, beyond the boundaries of your neighborhood, but it shouldn't be stressful. Giving should always bring joy to the giver, as well as the receiver.

My Journey into Christianity...
why?

"It is no longer I who live, but Christ who lives in me." (from Galatians 2:20)

"For you have died, and your life is hidden with Christ in God." (Colossians 3:3)

The above verses are often cited in the very peculiar Christian teaching that we should allow our human selves to die, so that God can live in us. I heard many sermons poetically suggesting that we die a little more each day. There should be less and less of our human nature, less of our desires and wants, feelings and emotions. It (or we) should slowly be replaced by the godly nature of Christ. We should take great joy in allowing ourselves to perish daily in this life, so that someday we could claim eternal life with Christ. But for some bizarre reason, it just didn't feel good to kill myself slowly for 10 years. I can't imagine why.

Some people are raised in church, and have never considered life outside the confines of Christianity. Others attend church occasionally, for holidays or baptisms, because it is a familiar tradition. Although the "casual believers" I've spoken with seem to have a healthier relationship with both religion and society, I can't speak to the emotional process involved with either of those extremes. Personally, I grew up free of religion, and made the conscious decision to submit myself to its convoluted and depressing grip as a mature, rational, well-educated adult.

Why?

When confronted with this question, I had to do some soul searching. My focus for the past several years, and while writing this book, had been on reasons to leave Christianity. I hadn't given much thought to why I *became* a Christian in the first place. I realized that I was an easy victim for the messages of Christianity. Having experienced a childhood that was often turbulent, less-than-ideal, and peppered with abuse, I readily related to the Christian notion that I am a helpless, worthless sinner, fully dependent on a savior. I felt so horrible about who I was, how unsuccessful, how foolish, how inept, that it was comforting to be in a huge sanctuary full of people who also professed regret about their own sinful and foolish nature. I related to feeling unloved, and was comforted by the message that all humans will fail you, and only God can offer strength and comfort. I felt unneeded, and took solace in the "great desire" God had for me, to serve his church, and help save the world. I related to the sense of an unfillable void, the striving and struggling to reach contentment. According to the Christian church, everyone had a void that only God could fill, and I would never be fully satisfied until I gave my life to him. All of this made sense to me. And because it made sense, I had my first foot in the door.

As a new believer, I liked the idea of challenging myself to become a better person, and Christianity seemed to encourage that. I also found comfort in the messages I heard weekly, on Sunday mornings. They may not have fazed a savvy and assertive, self-confident individual. But to little emotional, vulnerable me, the messages provided a deep, powerfully alluring comfort. It was a comfort reminiscent of being hugged, kissed, and tucked in at night, with the door left slightly ajar, so light would trickle in to make sense of shadows. The door ajar, because there is a promise that you are not alone. That someone is right outside the room, just far enough away as to be invisible, but near enough to come bursting in should you find yourself in a nightmare, or should you awaken, crying out. Come crashing through that narrowly open door, to flood the room with light and scare the monsters away.

The messages reminded me that I was a child, free of the heavy burden of interpreting reality and acting on it. I got to rest in the comfort of my father's choices. And this was a good parent, one who had my best interests at heart. One who knew me and loved me, just as I was. One who forgave me for every mistake I'd ever made, and offered a chance at total redemption.

This is the good parent, the perfect childhood, the warm fuzzies that the most hardened of grownups don't dare contemplate for long, at the risk of breaking to pieces.

And yet, you can have it all, if you just believe. Just say this prayer, silently, in your heart. The life you once had. Perhaps the life you never had. It's not too late. You are still my child.

These are the messages that seep in, seemingly innocuous, until you yearn for them like an addict for a fix.

Nothing can separate you from the love of God.

Everything that has ever happened to you was part of God's great plan for your life, and will ultimately lead to good.

You don't need to do anything to receive eternal life. It is given to you freely.

God will bless you richly, both in this life and in eternity. He has a perfect plan for your life, which will automatically materialize, if you stay in his will.

And perhaps the most captivating of all Christian notions:

One day, there will be no more sorrow, suffering, or pain. We will live in eternal bliss, with our loved ones, and with God. The bad will be punished, and the good rewarded. You have only to wait.

The idea that someday everything wrong will be made right and pain and sorrow will cease, is incredibly compelling. And (don't mind sayin') it's even more compelling when you *have* been wronged, and you *are* experiencing pain and sorrow. Couple that with a bunch of meditative music and some dry ice, and I'm pretty much ready to sign on the dotted line.

It wasn't all personal, either. The hope that the abused would some-day live in a paradise, where all pain is forgotten, got me through many a bitter news report. I also reveled in the very cool concept that the poor and the meek will inherit the Earth and everything in it. The rich hoity- toities will be brought down. The know-it-alls will find out that the people who never studied anything were smarter and greater than they were, all along. All good. All good. My (sorely missed) image of Hippie Jesus was well underway at this point.

I made sense out of the most horrible tragedies by letting that bedroom door burst open and spread light into my dark room, forming familiar shapes where there had been only a gnawing blackness. Horrible tragedies that plagued my mind suddenly had meaning, even something as tragic and senseless as a mur-dered child. Though I have never had to deal with something so devastating in my personal life, the mere thought of it hap-pening to another woman's child provokes an almost unbear-able pain in my heart. And I found that I could stop that pain by believing that the child was in a wonderful place, a glorious city, filled with love and joy. And I stopped that pain by believing that the unforgivable perpetrators of such a crime would suffer endlessly.

Is it not consoling?

The truth is that believing in religion doesn't reward victims, or punish criminals. It doesn't even help prevent crime. In fact, it has facilitated crimes, in particular those against youth, by employing its very curious power over us to second guess our internal compass and to put "God" or the church over the welfare of our own children. This unfounded trust in religious leaders and church members has led to the abuse of children, in many instances. And the equally inexplicable fear and respect demanded of church leaders has oftentimes prevented victims from seeking justice in their own lifetimes, let alone the false notion of postmortem retribution. So, while having blind faith may bring some superficial comfort, it actually adds to the likelihood of harm.

———

Even if I suspend reality and entertain the idea that the Bible is true, it doesn't really offer consolation. If I were to die and go to the Biblical heaven, I'd have to share it with The Yorkshire Ripper, the Son of Sam, and Jeffery Dahmer, all professed Christians. Meanwhile, any of their victims that hadn't given their life to Christ before their untimely death would be burning in eternal hell.

———

And yet, if I choose to believe, I will have the assurance of spending an eternity with my child, the person I love most on Earth. That was probably what kept me in the faith for many years after reality had resumed its hold on me. It is even comforting to look at the paintings, the statues, the beautiful depictions of angels, of a better place than this, and to revel in the notion that we'll live there together, forever. Admittedly, embracing the fact that I don't know if I'll see her again after I die has been the most challenging aspect of leaving Christianity, and I have yet to grapple with and overcome it. I believe I am just one of millions of people who, daily, allow the yearning for that comfort to override logic and reason.

While you are internalizing that rosy new reality, as a bonus, you are granted a whole new family who will love you while you are still here on Earth.

Being part of a church family was like being in a "normal" family, on steroids. It's a loving, embracing, caring, encouraging, warm, exciting, and HUGE family. They are there when you need a prayer, a shoulder to cry on, or someone to watch your kid. There are Thanksgiving dinners, and movie nights, and picnics, and conversations, and hot cocoa on cold mornings, and cookies. Lots of cookies. Your kids grow up together, and the other moms and dads are there to offer advice, and swap stories, and laugh, and cry.

Like a family, the church grows together, struggles together, feels pain together, works out problems together. It has its own history, and belief system, and approach to life, and you are a valued part of it. Your family also cares about the things you care about, feeding the hungry, blessing your neighbors, helping a person in need. You feel both valuable and valued in this family. You find ways to bring your unique talents into the family and use them for the family mission. This brings you and everybody else something exciting to look forward to and share regularly.

And you remember, for a moment, how worthless you felt when you were "outside."

Not only does it make sense, it makes sense of everything. It brings your life full circle. It explains away all of the terrible things that have ever happened to you. It remedies all the awful tragedies in the world, offering handfuls of redemption when applicable, or promises of retribution. It offers shelter from the storm, strength to endure life's bullets. It offers the best of loves, the kind that will never fade.

And insidiously, quietly, repetitively it reminds you

to die a little more, every day.

How I felt then, versus how I feel now...
hallelujah, I'm free!

Then: I spent 10 years as an adult Christian. Before this time, I was a very loving, accepting, non-judgmental and fun person. I had many friends, from all different walks of life. I studied world religions, as I have always felt connected to spirituality and the unknown. I was a songwriter, a story writer, a singer, an entrepreneur. I was in love with life, the ocean, trees, animals, people. I was confident in myself and my decisions, was successful in my career, and had a passion for adventure.

In my 10 years of Christianity, the light of those beautiful qualities was diminished. I began to loathe myself and view myself as an unworthy sinner. I felt that I was supposed to dedicate my life to God and in the process, I forgot to care about my own physical and financial well-being. I felt compelled to do things I wasn't comfortable with, such as "preaching" to those around me, and not accepting the uniqueness of others. This was SO not me! I was never able to come to terms with the belief that everybody else was going to hell. Since I didn't believe it, I never felt the desire to evangelize. However, I did get to the point of cutting back on relationships with people who were not Christian, but were fun, loving, progressive, intelligent and amazing people. Slowly many of my friendships withered, leaving me lonely and depressed.

I also began to severely limit my exposure to art, music, philosophy and science. I fell into the trap of questioning whether every song, every TV show, every game I played was "God honoring." I felt detached from life, afraid to participate in fully normal discussions, diversions, and relationships. It was an isolation and a depression unlike any I'd ever experienced. I didn't even know I was experiencing it. I just thought it was part of getting older, and of valuing eternity above the here and now. I never had the sensation that so many new converts describe, of wanting to run out and tell the world about how Jesus set them free. And thankfully, I never got to a point of condemning or criticizing the lifestyle choices of family members who are most dear to me.

After having my child, I lived immersed in fear. I was constantly afraid that something I did might cause her to suffer the consequences. I worried that God would retract his favor and somehow allow her to come to harm. My rational mind told me that God couldn't protect her from the real world, so I shied away from telling her that he would. At the same time, I was convinced that God, not science, was holding the world together, so there was nothing to give boundaries to my worries. When I questioned other Christians why God would allow horrible things to happen to children, the responses varied from, "Humans have free will," to "Satan has a lot of power on this Earth," to, "If God let his own son suffer and die a terrible death, I imagine He's fine with letting other people's children die." Or worse, "God takes people away from us to show us that He is the only eternal being, and we must love Him above all others." Consequently, I never let her out of my sight, believing that God could randomly, capriciously swipe her from me at any time, or allow Satan to bring her harm. (The whole Book of Job, which I still value for its poetic beauty, describes how God allows Satan to torment one of his faithful followers.) The Biblical God takes joy in causing calamity and anguish, not just to evildoers, but to the faithful, to "prove He is God." I am baffled when people profess consolation in the thought that God is in control of the universe!

In addition to depression and anxiety, it probably goes without saying that I was denied, and denied myself any human contact of a sexual or romantic nature. I felt awful, and prayed for forgiveness, if I experienced any such "temptation." I believed I was supposed to view all people as sons and daughters of God, and not experience any (completely normal) physical attraction to anyone. I rushed into marriage with the first person that expressed an interest, because I thought it was the only correct way to experience romance. Needless to say, the marriage was short lived, and was followed by several years of thinking myself unclean and unfit to try again. ('Cause the Bible tells me so.) During this entire time period, I belonged to a relatively progressive and liberal, non-denominational Christian church. I can't imagine how this process would be for someone in a strict, fundamentalist environment.

At 37, married, divorced, a single mom, I resigned myself to believing that I was worthless outside of serving God and living for my daughter. And though it sounds insane now, this thought was supposed to give me great joy. I was among God's chosen! I was blessed to live for God. The fact that it didn't bring me joy only deepened my confusion and sorrow. I spent years reading books on how to better myself as a mom, as a Christian, as a single woman. I never realized that my job wasn't to become better, or work harder. It was to appreciate how incredibly I was handling everything already. It was to realize that *I deserved to be happy, comfortable and well*, not that the world or God deserved a better version of me. My job should have been to seek out a better life for myself. Instead, I went to sleep every night thanking God for the scraps of love and slivers of joy that he tossed in my direction, and begged for forgiveness when I daydreamed of asking for more.

Before, I felt terribly indebted. I felt obligated to dedicate every spare moment and every spare dollar to this supreme being. A being that apparently thought I was worthless. A being that would not have allowed most of my close family and friends to spend eternity with me, even if it would have made me happy, as his joyous and faithful servant.

But Now: HALLELUJAH, I've been set free! I say that not to make light of the word, but because I truly feel it. Since my decision to leave Christianity, I have never had so much energy, such renewed passion for life, such excitement to see what lies ahead for me. I am thrilled to be able to raise my daughter in way that feels right to me. I am eager to love people again, the way I always had, without judgment, truly loving people for who they are. I crave the experiences I robbed myself of for so many years, music, books, relationships, spiritual moments that are not Christian in nature, but holistic. I also have a newfound love and appreciation for myself and for my life journey. I no longer harbor shame for who I have been, but admiration.

In fact, the things I was "supposed" to feel when I became a Christian (but never did) I feel now! Now is when I want to evangelize. I want to write about living free of religion! I want to talk about it! I feel alive, and free. My "sins" have been forgiven, because I have forgiven myself. I feel loved because I am sharing my true self with others. I feel embraced by life and the universe because I am not afraid to fall into its embrace. I feel like there's a purpose for everything. I feel empowered. I feel awakened. I wish I could share these feelings, these thoughts, these discoveries with the whole world. Maybe it took living as a Christian to truly value how amazing life is when you're not one.

One of the best things about not being Christian is not having to work so hard to bend and twist reality, to fit it into Biblical teaching. This has freed up so much mental energy, that I have become inspired to write and sing again. It's exhausting to invent so many excuses for God and Christianity, every single day! I felt like the wife who had to constantly reinvent her own reality, so she could go on loving her abusive husband.

I'm also wonderfully liberated from feeling like I should read the Bible, pray, go to church, volunteer at church, when I truly desired to dedicate that time to living life with my daughter, sharing time with other loved ones, being creative, exploring the country (and reading other things)! By not feeling forced into a Sunday morning regimen, I also feel like I have gained Saturday evening to have some quality time for myself. It may not seem like much, but as a single mom who works two jobs, simply having one night a week to stay up and watch a movie, and one morning to rest has made an indescribable difference in my state of mind and emotional well-being.

In addition to weekends, I have reclaimed my holidays. As a Christian, I felt it was my duty to spend Easter, Christmas Eve, Christmas, Mother's Day, and every other special occasion in church. I missed countless holidays with my non-religious family members. I turned down invitations to enjoy life with my loved ones. On many occasions, I drove my daughter to family gatherings, only to leave her alone with them while I spent the holiday serving my church. This year, I celebrated leaving Christianity by spending Easter with my father. He is over 80, and it was the first Easter I'd had with him since my childhood. How special it was to sit outside with him as my daughter ran through the yard looking for Easter eggs. I know it brought him many memories of when my sisters and I were children. My heart was full.

I will admit that forgoing the church routine does leave a schedule hole that takes some getting used to. As a person who was moderately involved in the church (one to two days a week), I did find myself missing the social time and the sense of belonging once I left. I can imagine that this sensation would be dreadfully acute for someone who was raised in church, or who was used to spending large chunks of their life in church or church-related activities. I am also fortunate in that many of my closest friends and family members are not of the religious persuasion, so I haven't had to severely alter my relationships and my free-time activities. It was more about re-involving them in my life. For me, leaving Christianity mainly consisted of stepping away from my church and my involvement with the church band, which I did enjoy and value. I have mad respect for those of you who are going through this journey in a more extreme way and finding it necessary to completely rewrite the structure of not only your spiritual life, but every pastime as well.

Depending on where you live, there may be some middle ground. For example, the UU Church (Unitarian Universalist) offers a church-like setting, while tolerating and teaching every belief system, including atheism. They are very socially active and offer many opportunities for their members to get plugged into serving society, without the pervading complexities of strict Christianity. A group called Sunday Assembly meets in some cities around the world. It is a "church" for people who don't believe in God, but still want the experience of helping others and seeking a sense of purpose. There are also many smaller ways to connect with likeminded individuals via local meetups, or through volunteer opportunities in the community. Consider ways in which you might use whatever talent you were lending to the church, to benefit a needy group of people. If you were teaching Sunday school, can you volunteer to read with foster kids? If you were singing on the worship team, can you join a local band that plays for free at community events? If you were an usher or a greeter, can you share that friendliness with lonely seniors at a retirement facility?

It's not all giving, of course. Church is also about receiving, and you don't want to leave yourself without a lifeline in times of need. It might become important for you to seek out the assistance and the company that you were receiving at church from other sources. Whenever possible, I would avoid continuing dependence on church-related assistance. Even if members of your previous church remain eager to visit you and help you, they will undoubtedly be holding onto hope that you'll "return to the fold." They will probably press you to converse about it, slip you casual hints and reminders, or even pressure you. You may end up feeling invaded and disrespected, which would stress the friendship. Although they have changed in some ways, I have maintained many of my friendships from church. However, when it comes to asking for help, I seek out family and friends that have no vested interest in convincing me to go to church with them.

Great new friends can be made: at community festivals, your local pub, demonstrations and marches, school events, volunteering, at a new part-time job, local races, marathons, or sporting events, camping, or classes at the YMCA. Libraries usually have several clubs that meet regularly and are free to join. There are meetups in most cities, everything from single moms, to singer-songwriters, book clubs, or simply adventure-seeking groups for every age. Lastly, it's fun to bond with neighbors. You may just find that while you were busy with church, many of them were planning awesome get togethers just down the street from where you live. Since leaving church, I have not had any significant downtime in which I felt lonely or bored. I have found great ways to utilize my time and amazing new friendships since I opened my heart and my schedule to the thousands of people outside of the church walls.

Do I have any regrets?

I've asked myself that question, and have concluded that I don't. I do realize that I missed time with friends, moments I excluded myself from because they did not live up to my high moral bar. Hypothetically, I missed unknown lovers I might have met, or unforgettable adventures I might have embarked on, or lessons I might have learned from nature, from life, from the world around me. There were shows I may have gone to, and songs I would have allowed myself to dance to. I know I would have loved myself more, cared for myself better. I'm sure my library would have been full of amazing books, and not one of them would have started with, "How to be a Better…"

In truth, though, I believe everything I've experienced in life has come together to make me who I am. And in fairness, I did have many wonderful Christian friendships and memorable moments at church services. Having lived inside and outside of Christianity, I have developed empathy for both sides, and maybe I can use that to write books like this one and help heal families. Maybe through my experience of leaving Christianity, I have learned how to stand up for the marginalized and the oppressed. Maybe my book can give a voice to those who have chosen not to partake in Christianity, but haven't had the ability or even the opportunity to explain why.

———

Most importantly, all the decisions in my life led me to who I am today. Because they led me to my daughter and to the joy I now feel, I wouldn't change a thing.

———

What I Believe...
and why I don't have to define it, or defend it.

There seems to be a general notion among Christians that you must have a clear and finalized belief regarding what will happen after you die. Otherwise, you will be wandering the earth void of any purpose, or any consolation. While I don't subscribe to that at all, I'd be happy to share how my thought process shifted and changed, as I was exiting organized religion.

My opinions about life after death vary, and I am pleasantly okay with that. Not knowing what is going to happen after I die has made every moment of my life exponentially more meaningful, not the other way around. I have found beauty and meaning in the song of birds, the cuddling of cats, laughter and silliness, walking in the sunshine, the sound of rain on the roof. Everything has meaning, because it is a beautiful decoration of this moment, a moment that will never return. Since I am no longer filling my hours with the fear of displeasing God, or with a desperate search to live purposefully in the Christian sense, I have found that life and time itself is significant enough. My purpose is to be me, to be here. To extend love and care to those around me through being respectful to myself and to others, and allowing myself to feel unbridled happiness.

I enjoy learning about the philosophies and beliefs of others. It adds wonder and amazement to my life to entertain the notions of spirits, reincarnation, life after death, eternal rest, or even a scientific infinity. **I will also add that I am much more comfortable accepting that there might not be a heaven, than I ever was believing in the existence of hell.**

I don't need to have the answers, to have a full and fruitful life. I rest in the thought that this life matters. It truly matters. We can impact our Earth, our loved ones, the people, animals, and plants we share this time and place with. I also know, from science, that matter is neither created nor destroyed. We are all eternal. The atoms that built us have been in existence forever, and will be forevermore, in all of their various forms and purposes. We have been stars. We have been water. We have been trees. We have been sky. And we will be these things again. I don't need a god-figure to encourage me to behave well, or make healthy choices. I do those things because I love myself and those around me. I also don't need the threat of punishment to feel sorrow or regret for mistakes I've made. In fact, opting to treat others with the respect they deserve is a much more authentic kindness than basing your actions on what "God" commands or threatens.

Sometimes I think our consciousness ends at death, and I'm all right with that. It would be much more restful than continuing on through life's struggles, again and again. And yet, I can't help but imagine that everything I know as life is only a mere sliver of what is to come. It seems more logical that, as incredibly complex as our life is, there are unfathomable complexities beyond the physical restraints of our own planet, our own physical bodies and minds. It would make sense to me that if there is something after death, it would be exponentially more difficult to outline and depict than our current world is. Therefore, the very rudimentary descriptions of heaven in the Bible don't seem fitting at all.

The closest real-world analogy I can come up with is Minecraft. When I watch my daughter play Minecraft, I wonder if we are trapped in a similar state of existence. There are those within the game, and those outside of it, in "the real world," an infinite space and time that goes beyond the confines of the Minecraft code. The characters in Minecraft are doomed to obey the natural and physical laws of their world. There are consequences for their choices and actions. If they could rationalize, they would believe their world to be complex and multi-dimensional, having a past, present, and future. They would experience free will and an almost endless array of possible choices, as well as random acts of nature, much as we do on Earth. And yet, their world is only two dimensional (or less, considering that it is wholly comprised of dimension-less lines of code). We can stop and restart their world hundreds of times, or go back to any point in their past, and they'd never even know it! Their world is only a minuscule and malleable sliver of the "real world," the "outside world."

I guess I like to think of the life we know as code. I'll concede that there is a chance, perhaps, that this code is written by a creator, and that another creator wrote the code for our creator. It could just as likely have been spawned by a universe outside of our own. It could be an experiment, or part of a continuum where those who live in one universe create the next universe. (We have, for example, already created the universe of cyberspace.)

I believe life as we know it is a tiny, but important level of infinite planes of existence. Regardless of the concept of a soul, our physical matter and the elements that reside in us will reside infinitely in our own universe. Maybe the marks we leave in our own lifetimes set infinite ripples in motion, affecting everything to come. Our genes, our memories, our footprints creating new paths, new outcomes, new possibilities. Thereby, we would also achieve some level of eternal life, in a more esoteric sense.

When it comes to religious practices, my daughter and I still pray now and then. But we don't pray for specific blessings for ourselves or others. We don't ask God to rescue animals, or save souls, or help the poor. We simply take a moment to express gratitude for the experiences of the day, the time we shared, the things we accomplished, the food we ate. Then we ask that our hearts be filled with peace and rest for the night, and close in the name of the Great Love of the Universe. More than anything, this "prayer" is a way of remembering and verbally recognizing the joys of a day well lived. It is then followed by a conscious and verbal transition into a restful state, in preparation for sleep, and an acknowledgement of love.

The key to this chapter, both in my book and in my life, is that I no longer have to believe that I know the answer. I can live freely in the full truth that neither I, nor anyone, knows what happens after death. I am also relinquished from claiming to others that I know the answer. (Or worse, telling them that their very own beautiful, cultural, personal understanding of life and eternity is wrong.) Lastly, I relish the liberty that comes from understanding that I absolutely do not owe anyone an explanation for my beliefs, or for my lack thereof. I don't need to defend my innermost, personal thoughts, choices, or comprehension of the meaning of life. That is mine, and no one has a right to invade it, micromanage it, or ridicule it.

I hope, dear reader, that you embrace your own inherent freedom to study, learn, choose, believe, sense, yearn, and reach for your very own understanding. This is, potentially, the most valuable gift of being alive: being yourself and continuing to grow daily.

The Challenge...

how to love others, when they're saying horrible things to you.

It took me years of study, both religious and secular, to define where I stood on the topic of Christianity. After I made my choice, I faced several months of even more harrowing decisions.

Should I stay in church?

Should I tell people?

How can I tell people?

Will they still love me? Will they let my daughter play with their kids? Will they try to convince my daughter, behind my back, to continue believing in Jesus? Will they be accepting of my inherent right to choose my own belief system, and move on to conversing about other things? Or will our every conversation from now until I die be an overt attempt to change my mind, to the point of exasperation, and void of any other quality?

Will I feel bullied, or maybe unheard? And if so, will I yell, cower, or say things I'll regret?

What's the best way to talk about something that is so very, very emotionally charged?

These questions eventually led me to page one of *Love over Religion*. I decided I would simply write down my reasons for leaving Christianity. I would then keep a copy and send it to anyone who asked me the question. It would be my readily-available damage control. It would be nonconfrontational, maybe even superficial, and five pages, at best.

I bet you agree with me now, that it is none of the above! The wonderful thing is that it is a letter not just to one or two people. It has become a letter to anyone who wants to read it, not just my friends and family, but yours as well.

I wish that I could go on your very specific journey with you, but I cannot. What I can do is share how it went for me, when it was time to "come out" to family and friends. I can offer you the comfort of knowing that life is complex and love can prevail, no matter where you stand on the topic of Christianity. I can offer you my "letter," and I do hope you will use it as if it were your very own.

When the time came for me, I chose to first talk to friends and family members that I knew would be on my side. If you are also on this journey, I would encourage you to do the same. It is important for two reasons. One, you will have a difficult road ahead of you for a while, so you might as well have some people in your corner, rooting you on. And two, those people have been waiting to hear this good news for a long time, so why keep it from them another day? It felt so amazing to be "welcomed back" by certain friends and family members who had never understood my choice to become religious (although they were kind enough to support my journey, throughout.) I could see the relief in their eyes, and I knew I had not lost too much time. There were still adventures ahead, and memories to make with the real me.

An important step was talking to my pastor and friend. He had always been inspirational to me, modeling what religion should look like. He had stepped in, on many occasions, to help me both financially and emotionally. He even took it upon himself to invite my daughter to the Daddy-Daughter dances at school, along with his own girls, so that she wouldn't have to miss out on them. I treasured those kind gestures. We had shared many moments and conversations. His wife and I were friends, and our children played together at every opportunity. I feared divulging my true feelings about Christianity to these cherished friends, to the point of losing sleep for months. Not only was I afraid of losing their friendship. I was also afraid of hurting their feelings, after they had shown me such kindness.

———

It isn't like me to go around stabbing people where it hurts the most, and I felt like I would be doing that every time I shared my views with a devout Christian.

———

I addressed my change of heart in an email. I was overjoyed and even cried, when both he and his wife offered me a loving and accepting reply. They even expressed sadness that I had gone through so much time alone, worrying about what I was going to say to them. They assured me that they would listen, judgment-free, to any spiritual anxieties I was going through. When we got together in person, they both encouraged me to talk about my decision. My pastor expressed his (completely understandable) hope that I would change my mind, but he was also firm about his commitment to accept me and love me, no matter what I chose. He said that my daughter and I would be welcome in their lives, unconditionally, and that they wouldn't have it any other way. It felt wonderful to be accepted, if not completely understood.

The rockiest road was yet to come, as I prepared to talk to the most religious members of my family. When at last the time came (and trust me, there is never a good time), I equipped myself with the book I had written. I referenced verses, and paused to read, trying (and sometimes failing) to keep a calm, confident pace. I edified my own stance with the research I'd done, and I was thrilled that I could use it as a crutch every time daggers like this were hurled at me:

You and all of your siblings are going to hell.

You are obviously a Baal worshiper.

You are going to miss out on an opportunity to spend eternity with God.

You deserve all of the terrible things that are going to happen to you.

I guess it was nice to see that my concerns about hurting people's feelings were completely one sided, in my own favor. It allowed me to unleash my true feelings. I realized that I didn't even need to have rebuttals lined up, if I simply occupied my rightful space. At that point, I had the microphone and, quite frankly, the dagger-hurlers couldn't get a word in edge-wise. And that's okay.

———

They hadn't let anyone get a word in edge-wise for centuries. It was my turn to speak.

———

Unlike my fears suggested, after I had this conversation I felt accomplished, invigorated, and clean. I felt younger, and fearless. And best of all, nothing had changed. I was still me. My religious family members and friends were still who they are. We still loved one another. I can even say that my love for certain family members grew, after I discussed my position. Upon standing my ground and claiming my space, I was suddenly aware of *their vulnerability* instead of my own. It made sense even to feel sorry for them. After all, as I had been misled by religion, so were they. The only difference was, they had not escaped its grip.

Once I achieved this sense of sympathy, years of anxiety over family relationships seemed to wash away. I was free to be me, but I was also free to love them for who they were. I no longer had the pressure to believe what they believed and therefore, I could love them. I could understand why they chose to believe it and still, very confidently, refuse to believe it myself.

I haven't spoken to every person in my life about this yet. What matters is that I feel equipped to, if and when necessary, both to establish boundaries and to share who I am and what I believe, with whomever cares to learn about me. I have even shared my book with total strangers, when approached in an "evangelical" way. If they genuinely want to know what I think, then I genuinely want to share. In fact, I am honored when any person wants to learn a little bit about my path, my journey, the things I have learned in this life. Shouldn't we all be learning from one another? If we could, our own lives would be enhanced, and the world would be a better, more peaceful place to reside.

Today, I told my dad about my beliefs and about the book I'm writing. He is not Christian and he didn't address any of the religious concerns. However, he expressed immediate worry that I would be putting myself in jeopardy. "I hope this is only going to be online," he said. "Very religious people might get upset, and I wouldn't want people showing up at your house or anything."

————

I think it's pretty telling that (in a free country and in the year 2017) a father would worry about his daughter's safety, if she publicly rejected Christianity.

————

Now, if you are a Christian, and somebody tells you that they are leaving Christianity, you will probably toss the following phrases at them, before you do much thinking. I am basing this on my personal experience, and on conversations I've had with others. (And here's looking at YOU, nonbeliever, as you prepare a savvy answer to the following.)

1. You never knew the Lord, or you wouldn't leave.

    You're right. Luckily, I never knew God during my religious phase, but I do now. I've read the Bible and done some research, and I realize that he has traits that I can't reconcile with a loving god.

    I knew the Lord that I wanted to believe in, and he will always be in my heart, the loving, wholly good, powerful protector. Unfortunately, Christian scripture does not line up with the beautiful religious experience I had, and I choose to base my decision on what the Bible truly says, not on my feelings.

Actually, you don't know the Lord either. All either of us has is a concept of him, based on what we've learned, what we've read, and our own ruminations.

2. You have the choice to live forever in heaven, and you are choosing hell.

I have no desire to spend eternity with anyone who has committed genocide, allowed women to be persecuted, demanded animal sacrifice, or killed their own child.

If you truly believe the Bible, there is no choice. Our lives are planned by God from the time we are in the womb. Which, by the way, includes whether or not we will be born, or be aborted, and exactly how many days we'll live. (Psalm 139:16)

The Bible says the dead are judged according to their deeds, not on their beliefs. (Revelation 20:12, Romans 2:6, Proverbs 24:12, Matthew 7:21)

Since I don't believe in heaven or hell after death, that statement is meaningless to me. I do, however, wish to avoid a life of hell on earth. Being untrue to myself, especially when it comes to loving and accepting myself and others, would feel like a living hell.

3. The enemy has tricked you into losing faith. He's lying to you.

   I don't hear voices. Do you?

   Actually, my decision was based fully on the "word of God."

   I haven't lost faith. I've proudly lost organized religion.

   Since I don't believe that there are a bunch of hobgoblins waging war on God for my eternal soul, that statement is meaningless to me.

4. This isn't over. We need to work this out.

   I am happy to continue the conversation, under the very clear understanding that my thoughts and opinions are just as valid as yours. If you refuse to accept that, there is no need to converse further.

   Don't make your life a living hell by worrying about what's going to happen to me after I die. Let's enjoy life while we're here together.

   I have made a decision. If your ultimate purpose is to win souls for Christ, you'll be more successful talking to someone who is undecided. But I'm happy to talk with you, about other things.

I agree that this isn't over. Nothing is permanent and we should all have wiggle room in our philosophies.

I am willing to talk to you, as long as it takes, to open your eyes to reality. Just know that it might be painful.

5. Certain Bible verses aren't politically correct, and you probably feel the pressure of society to be more accepting.

I'm less concerned with a specific verse or two, than I am with the appalling lack of morality expressed throughout the entire Bible.

Christians are not consistent in how they handle "delicate subject matter." The Bible is just as adamant about divorce, hairstyles, and women's inequality, as it is about homosexuality and extramarital sex.

Even though I have many reasons to leave Christianity, I agree that discrimination is a huge one, and may be top on my list. If we both concede that Christianity practices discrimination, that lends credibility to my point, not yours.

The fact that the Bible, which is supposedly written by a loving God, talks about sending groups of people to hell, is enough to prove that it is false, as far as I'm concerned.

6. But Jesus came to change all of that. (Every time you mention anything in the Old Testament.)

I think Jesus is pretty cool, and I wish so much that he had started his very own religion, instead of aligning himself to the religion of the Old Testament. Unfortunately, he does claim to be one and the same as the God who committed what I consider to be atrocities. Therefore, I can't accept or believe that Jesus is a true god.

If God were real, there wouldn't have been any need to send someone to change his laws. God never had to establish cruel and unnecessary rules such as animal or human sacrifice in the first place, much less allow it to go on for thousands of years, before putting a stop to it.

The fact that all of the prophesies and their fulfillments are part of the same book, is evidence to me that it is a falsified document. If you can show me sources outside of the Bible that corroborate the story of Jesus, or the many uncanny prophesies that came to pass, I'd be more inclined to lend it some credence.

I'm sure that there are many other comments, knee-jerk reactions, that I have yet to hear. It is wise to be prepared with a calm, but firm answer. Devout Christians have prepared and rehearsed the things they say. They study, hear weekly messages, and learn the most powerful ways to convince people that Christianity is the one true religion. If their statements come off as void of emotion, or thoughtless, it is because they are! I don't mean this in an insulting way. Christians are simply regurgitating what they have repetitively heard. They are often desensitized to the true meaning behind the messages, and even the cruelty inherent in them. I participated in Christianity and I know how the phrases take hold and begin to sound true. This is why I don't think it's wrong to prepare and rehearse some responses. In fact, it's a great way to keep emotions at bay. Your relationships with loved ones are valuable. To preserve relationships, it's helpful to carry on a debate using logic and reason, and not get tied up in the hurt and anger.

Finally, it is good to remember that Christians genuinely feel they are throwing you a lifeline. Sure, by the time it reaches your ears it might sound like, "You're a stupid devil worshipper, and you're going to burn in hell."

Try to hear this:

> "I love you. I've been misled into believing that this is the best way I can show you love. I care about you enough to want to spend eternity with you. If I didn't want you in my life forever, I wouldn't be having this conversation at all. I'm sorry that our relationship has suffered, but in my perspective, this part of our rela-tionship (here on Earth) is brief, temporary, and mean-ingless in comparison to what is yet to come. So I'm

willing to lose your love and friendship now, if I can do everything I can to guarantee your eternal safety and joy. Plus, I'm doing this because somebody convinced me that hell is real, and I'm afraid."

It's hard.

Try.

I have named this final chapter "The Challenge," but it is not for the reason you may think. Yes, my journey out of Christianity was a challenge, in many ways. It challenged my intellect to research and learn about the harmful aspects of Christianity. It challenged my emotions to hear words that hurt and insulted me, and to force myself to see through them. It is challenging to stand up for my beliefs, and to stand up for the oppressed. It is also challenging to remember those who have been wronged, marginalized, harmed, killed by those who claim to be God's chosen people. It hurts, deeply, to even think about those people. It was a tremendous challenge to find the courage to write this book, to present it to those closest to me. It will be an even greater challenge to take the plunge and release it into the world. And certainly, I've braced for the many challenges that will come knocking on my door (figuratively, Dad.) as soon as I do.

But the purpose of this chapter, and this whole book, is not to tell you about what challenged me. It is to propose a challenge, to you.

I challenge you, my Christian reader, to continue reading, learning, listening and opening your heart to the thoughts of others. Consider and study beliefs that oppose your own, if only to broaden your awareness. I challenge you to embrace the difficult truth that Christian beliefs are opinions, and they hold equal value to the opinions of others. Nobody knows what happens after we die. I challenge you to take a stand against the discrimination of others, over religion, while we live.

I challenge you, non-believer, ex-believer, questioning-believer, to be true to yourself. However it translates to your circumstance, be strong and brave in the face of religious pressure. Know that you are not alone. Even if everyone in your immediate circle is Christian, there are billions of people worldwide who are not. You, like everyone else, have the right to fill your heart as you see fit, to share it, and to love in the way you choose. I challenge you to continue learning from all walks of human wisdom, gleaning from its vastness everything that brings meaning, hope, joy, and peace into your life.

I challenge all of us to keep the conversation going, to never turn our backs on one another, and in this way…

to choose love, over religion.

To loved ones who have supported my ideals,
in spite of their own.

References

A quick note: I made the unorthodox choice not to list Bible versions after every verse I quoted. I did this to streamline reading and to encourage cross-referencing and further study. I intentionally drew from several versions of the Bible. Churches I've attended also draw from various Bible versions, and tend to use whichever one illustrates the point of their message most clearly. Typing the chapter name and verse number into a search engine will bring up every version of it, for comparison. Since all scripture is God-breathed (2 Timothy 3:16), I trust that any variations across versions are insignificant (wink wink).

1. Sean Gregory, "Donald Trump Dismisses his 'Locker Room Talk' as normal. Athletes Say it's Not." *Time Sports* (October 2016)

2. United States Department of Justice Archives. https://www.justice.gov/archives/opa/blog/updated-definition-rape

3. https://biblicalgenderroles.com/2015/07/11/is-my-husband-raping-me/

4. NCADV. (2015). Facts about domestic violence and sexual abuse. Retrieved from www.ncadv.org

5. Katheryn Joyce, "Biblical Battered Wife Syndrome: ChristianWomen and Domestic Violence." (June 18, 2 009) http://religiondispatches.org/biblical-battered-wife-syndrome-christian-women-and-domestic-violence/

6. Bullying Statistics – Anti-bullying Help, Facts, and More http://www.bullyingstatistics.org/content/gay-bullying-statistics.html

7. "The Religious Right's War on LGBT Americans" *Americans United for Separation of Church and State* https://www.au.org/resources/publications/the-religious-rights-war-on-lgbt-americans

8. Wikipedia, the Free Encyclopedia (July 2017) https://en.wikipedia.org/wiki/Animal_sacrifice

9. Barry Davenport, "30 Signs of Emotional Abuse." *Live Bold and Bloom* http://liveboldandbloom.com/11/relationships/signs-of-emotional-

10. "The Science of Desire," *Independent* (September 2008) http://www.independent.co.uk/life-style/love-sex/desire/the-science-of-desire-933969.html#

And check out a Christian article on this same topic: Juli Slattery, "Sex is a Physical Need," *Focus on the Family* (2009) http://www.focusonthefamily.com/marriage/sex-and-

intimacy/understanding-your-husbands-sexual-needs/
sex-is-a-physical-need

11. Christopher Ryan, Ph.D. "Sexual Repression: The Malady that Considers Itself the Remedy." *Psychology Today* (April 2010) https://www.psychologytoday.com/blog/sex-dawn/201004/sexual-repression-the-malady-considers-itself-the-remedy

12. Wikipedia, the Free Encyclopedia (June 2017) https://en.wikipedia.org/wiki/Flood_myth

13. To explore some of the astonishing similarities between Jesus and Osiris, check out Ernest Moyer's "Studies in the Origins of the Ancient Egyptian People." http://www.egyptorigins.org/index.html

14. For an in-depth look at how Jim Jones used "faith" to abuse and murder his followers, try Rose Wunrow's "The psychological massacre: Jim Jones and People's Temple, an Investigation." http://jonestown.sdsu.edu/?page_id=29478

15. Christine Wicker, "Dumbfounded by Divorce," *The Dallas Morning News* (2000) http://www.adherents.com/largecom/baptist_divorce.html

16. Jeanna Bryner, "Teen Birth Rates Higher in Highly Religious States," *Live Science* (September 2009) http://

www.livescience.com/5728-teen-birth-rates-higher-highly-religious-states.html

17. Paul Coughlin, "Pornography and Virtual Infidelity," *Focus on the Family* (2009) http://www.focusonthefamily.com/marriage/divorce-and-infidelity/pornography-and-virtual-infidelity/virtual-infidelity-and-marriage

18. Jennifer Dunning, "Religious Believers more Depressed than Atheists, Study" *Your Community Blog* (September 2013) http://www.cbc.ca/newsblogs/yourcommunity/2013/09/religious-believers-more-depressed-than-atheists-study.html

19. Susie Allen, "Religious upbringing associated with less altruism, study finds," *U Chicago News* (November 2015) https://news.uchicago.edu/article/2015/11/05/religious-upbringing-associated-less-altruism-study-finds

20. Chuck Colson, "Domestic Violence within the Church, the Ugly Truth," *Christian Headlines* (October 2009)http://www.christianheadlines.com/news/domestic-violence-within-the-church-the-ugly-truth-11602500.html

21. Annie Waldman, "Study: Religious children are less able to distinguish fantasy from reality" BBC News (July, 2014) http://www.bbc.com/news/blogs-echochambers-28537149

22. Zaid Jilani, "Despite Wingnut Freakout, Obama is Right: Christian Violence is Just as Bad as Muslim Violence." *AlterNet* (February 2015) http://www.alternet.org/belief/despite-wingnut-freakout-obama-right-christian-violence-just-bad-muslim-violence

23. Alex Henderson, "6 Modern-day Christian terrorist groups our media conveniently ignores." *AlterNet* (April 2015) http://www.salon.com/2015/04/07/6_modern_day_christian_terrorist_groups_our_media_conveniently_ignores_partner/

24. Greg Laden, "How many people were killed as Witches in Europe, from 1200 to the present?" *Science Blogs* (December 2012)

25. "Mystic Voices, The Story of the Pequot War." http://www.pequotwar.com/history.html

26. "Army of God letters support accused bomber Eric Rudolph." *CNN.com/US* (March 2002)

27. Maia Szalavitz, "Investigative Report Reveals Some Religious Reform Schools are Havens for Child Abuse." *Time* (November 2012)

28. Jamie Manson, "The Orthodox Church's Role in Russia's Anti-gay Laws." *National Catholic Reporter* (August 2013)

https://www.ncronline.org/blogs/grace-margins/
orthodox-church-s-role-russia-s-anti-gay-laws

29. Charity Navigator, Your Guide to Intelligent Giving."
https://www.charitynavigator.org/index.cfm/bay/content.
view/cpid/42

30. Derek Beres "How to make $71 Billion a Year: Tax the
Churches" *Big Think* (2017) http://bigthink.com/21st-century-
spirituality/how-to-make-71-billion-a-year-tax-the-churches

31. Wikipedia, *"Supplemental Nutrition
Assistance Program."* https://en.wikipedia.org/wiki/
Supplemental_Nutrition_Assistance_Program

32. Remy Melina, "The Surprising Truth: Christians Once
Banned Christmas." *Live Science* (December 2010) https://
www.livescience.com/32891-why-was-christmas-banned-in-
america-.html

33. M.J. Alexander, "Dance Fever: The Town that I
nspired (and Got) Footloose." *405 Magazine* (Jun
e 2015) http://www.405magazine.com/June-2015/
Dance-Fever-The-Town-That-Inspired-and-Got-Footloose/

34. Alan Hanson, "Elvis History Blog." (February 2011) http://
www.elvis-history-blog.com/elvis-religious-criticism.html

35. To explore the enactment and repealing of Blue Laws throughout history, check out, "What are Blue Laws?" *Today I Found Out, Feed Your Brain* (December 2014) http://www.todayifoundout.com/index.php/2014/12/blue-laws-come/

36. Wikipedia "Sunday Football in Northern Ireland." https://en.wikipedia.org/wiki/Sunday_football_in_Northern_Ireland

37. Wikipedia "Religious Debates over the *Harry Potter* Series." https://en.wikipedia.org/wiki/Religious_debates_over_the_Harry_Potter_series

38. Tim Chivers, "North Carolina church plans Halloween Bible Burning." *The Telegraph* (October 2009) http://www.telegraph.co.uk/news/religion/6346662/North-Carolina-church-plans-Halloween-Bible-burning.html

39. Tom Batchelor, "Christian-run cinema refuses to show *Beauty and the Beast* for having gay character." *Independent* (March 2017)

40. Benedict Carey "Long-awaited Medical Study Questions the Power of Prayer" *The New York Times* (March, 2006) http://www.nytimes.com/2006/03/31/health/31pray.html

41. Gayle A. Sulik M.A., Ph.D. "Cause Marketing is not Philanthropy" *Psychology Today* (October 2013) https://www.psychologytoday.com/blog/pink-ribbon-blues/201310/cause-marketing-is-not-philanthropy

42. Timothy Ogden "Why Cause Marketing Can Actually Backfire" *Forbes* (January 2011) https://www.forbes.com/2011/01/12/cause-marketing-backfire-leadership-cmo-network-strategies.html

43. "4 Questions Before You Buy Pink" Think Before You Pink.org http://thinkbeforeyoupink.org/resources/before-you-buy/

44. http://thinkbeforeyoupink.org/past-campaigns/

45. See, for example: http://www.cnn.com/2010/WORLD/americas/01/21/religion.mega.church.christian/

    http://www.newsweek.com/2013/10/25/are-churches-making-america-poor- 243734.html

46. Church Tithing #Best Hustle Ever (July 2012) http://bwwrites.com/?p=352

Made in the USA
Columbia, SC
30 January 2021